W9-BQX-074

Personality Type in Congregations

How to Work with Others
More Effectively

Lynne M. Baab

An Alban Institute Publication

All biblical quotations are from the New Revised Standard Version of the Bible, copyright © 1989 by Oxford University Press, New York.

Quotations in the section "God" in chapter 1 are taken from *Pray Your Way* by Bruce Duncan, published and copyright 1993 by Darton, Longman and Todd Ltd. and used by permission of the publishers.

Myers-Briggs Type Indicator and MBTI are registered trademarks of Consulting Psychologists Press, Inc., Palo Alto, California.

Library of Congress Catalog Card Number 97-78129
ISBN 1-56699-193-5

CONTENTS

ACKNOWLEDGMENTS

I want to convey my thanks to many helpful people who talked with me about type in congregations, particularly Nathaniel Pierce, Barbara Pursey, Marie Sheldon, and Maureen Jesnik. I'm grateful for wonderful conversations with Bruce Duncan about prayer, the shadow, spirituality, and type. I want to thank the many fascinating people with whom I spoke on the phone and at the Association for Psychological Type (APT) international meetings during my years as APT Interest Area Consultant. Without those conversations this book never would have been written. I also want to thank Patti Holman and Nancy Ross who first introduced me to type and with whom I have endlessly discussed type and faith. I'm very grateful to my editor, Beth Ann Gaede, and to Fred Wagner, both of whom provided so many helpful suggestions for this book.

The phone rang.

A United Methodist layperson from halfway across the country was calling for advice. "I've just completed the training to administer the Myers-Briggs Type Indicator," he said. "I'd like to use it in my church."

"In what area were you thinking about using type?" I asked. "Prayer? There are a number of ways you can think about prayer in the light of type. Are you interested in helping people find a place to serve in your congregation? Type can help you there. You could use type lots of other ways, too: parenting classes, spiritual direction, working with the leaders of the congregation. . . . What did you have in mind?"

"I'm interested in all of those," he answered.

"Do you have a paper and pencil?" I said. "I can tell you the names of a couple of great books on type and prayer. Then there are some others about using type to find a place to serve. A couple of books deal with type and church leadership."

"Great."

For four years—from 1993 to 1997—I got one or two phone calls like that every month. During those years I served on the Interest Area Council of the Association for Psychological Type (APT). My area of responsibility was religious and spiritual issues. Each quarter I wrote a column for the newsletter published by APT. In that newsletter my phone number was listed so members could call and ask questions.

I got calls from people wanting to use type in their personal spiritual lives. I got calls from people wanting to use type in their Buddhist communities or in synagogues. The majority of calls came from Christians, both lay leaders and pastors, who wanted to use type in their congregations.

I often wished I could refer them to a single book that would present an overview of all the ways type could be used in a congregation. This book was born out of that wish.

My Own Story

When I first learned about type in 1986, it was marvelously freeing. My type preferences are for introversion, intuition, thinking, and judging (INTJ), and because the American culture of my childhood in the 1950s and 1960s seemed to value extraversion and sensing, I always felt that something was wrong with me.

I am gregarious and friendly, so my friends often can't discern whether I'm an extravert or introvert. As soon as I understood that introversion and extraversion refer to the source or direction of energy, I knew I was an introvert. I am energized by my own reflections and thoughts, and I am fatigued by contact with the outer world. This always felt like some kind of abnormality. That's probably why I worked so hard to develop extraverted skills and learned to connect easily with people.

Psychological type gave me the language to describe some of my uniqueness in positive terms. I could begin to dare to hope that God had made me an introvert for a purpose. Maybe it was even true that God took pleasure in my being an introvert. Maybe it was a good and wonderful thing, different perhaps from the more preferred pattern of human behavior, but valuable nonetheless. Perhaps I might even have a special contribution to make because I am an introvert.

Having the language to describe intuition was helpful in the same way. In my birth family everyone besides me preferred sensing. I have always been ashamed of being dreamy, reflective, and untidy. The pockets of my bathrobes are usually ripped because I catch them on doorknobs. I often have mysterious bruises because I'm always bumping into things. The physical world has never been as real to me as my own thoughts, particularly my thoughts of possibilities and concepts. Again, after learning about type, I found myself thinking that maybe God had given me intuition as a gift, a good and wonderful gift, but a gift that's not shared by the majority in our society who prefer the world of the concrete and tactile.

Within months of my first exposure to personality type I understood there must be faith implications related to type. I had already experienced the joy of increased self-acceptance through understanding the

differences among people, and I had gained a sense of God's delight in
the way I'm made. My mind was bursting with other possibilities. For
more than a decade I'd been teaching the New Testament material on
spiritual gifts. I wondered if type could be correlated with spiritual gifts.
I came across *Prayer and Temperament*,[1] at that time one of the only
books available that related type to spirituality. I began thinking about
type and prayer.

I also began wondering if type could help explain people's preferences in their congregations. Do introverts prefer quiet activities while
extraverts like fellowship events? I asked questions and ultimately did
a small research project as a part of my seminary education. I attended
training to administer the Myers-Briggs Type Indicator (MBTI). I also
taught classes in congregations on spiritual gifts and psychological type.

In 1993 I saw an advertisement requesting applications for the position of Interest Area Consultant for the Association for Psychological
Type in the area of religious and spiritual issues. I was chosen to fill that
role. In addition to writing a quarterly column and receiving phone calls,
I organized symposia on religious and spiritual issues for the APT international meetings in 1995 and 1997. I met many fascinating people at
the international conferences and over the phone. My conversations with
them were wonderful. Those conversations gave me many of the ideas
you'll find in this book.

Type as One Tool

Learning about type was revolutionary for me, a giant "Aha!" experience. While acknowledging my great debt in this area, I also want to
affirm that type is only one tool for understanding personality and it is
only one tool to encourage growth in faith. It is a helpful and insightful
tool, but it is not equivalent to the Gospel itself, nor is it the only source
of wisdom about people or the only guide to spiritual growth.

I'm sure you know the story of the blind men and the elephant. Each
man had a hold on a different part of the elephant. One man thought the
elephant was like a tree because he held onto a leg. Others held onto the
trunk, the tail, and the side of the elephant, and they each drew a separate conclusion.

I view human personality as an unbelievably complex sculpture.

Type gives us a snapshot from one vantage point. It is a very useful snapshot, but it is just one view. The view from other angles points up other issues and characteristics, just as the men holding on to the elephant's tail, leg, and trunk had different views of the elephant.

Type does not address issues of birth order. Countless studies have explored the influence of birth order on our personalities and convictions.[2] It is no surprise to me, based on what I've read, that as a firstborn I am deeply committed to the institution of the church. In general INTJs are independent and self-directed. That is true for me to some extent, but as a firstborn, I am fairly conventional and not very rebellious against the institutions of society.

Type does not address intensity. My older son and I are very intense, passionate people. My younger son and my husband are much milder in manner, yet most INTJs I meet are more mild than intense. I believe intensity is an inherited characteristic that is independent of type.

Type does not address fears or insecurities. People of all types can be anxious, concerned, and worried when under stress, and people of all types can be generally self-confident and calm. Perhaps this anxiety/calmness continuum is related to what I call intensity, but I experience these emotions as being different. My intense, passionate son and I are both quite self-confident.

Type is not the same as spiritual gifts. I will address spiritual gifts at length later, but I will say now that I have become convinced that the material in the New Testament on spiritual gifts presents a vantage point other than type from which to view human giftedness. There is some overlap, but not a lot. Spiritual gifts are important to learn about. For some people, understanding spiritual gifts will be the most helpful key to effective service; for others, type will provide that insight. Some people will benefit equally from knowing about both, because each seems to touch on different issues.

What Type Can Do

Type is a helpful lens through which to view prayer and personal connection with God. Understanding type can help us observe patterns of prayer that are comfortable for us, and type can help us experiment with new forms of prayer that can stretch us. Understanding type can help us discern some of the ways we grow spiritually over the life cycle. Type can give us vocabulary to describe the journey of faith. But the work of the Holy Spirit in us is complex indeed, and I would never want to say that everything God does in us can be described through the lens of type.

Type can help us evaluate congregational activities. It is tempting to say that we need to be sure we schedule quiet events for introverts and large social events for extraverts. I want to propose that everyone needs times of quiet and times of sociability. In fact, at our church many extraverts attend the contemplative prayer events. All of us function in both the introverted and extraverted worlds, and we will see that in fact we may meet God most dramatically in our least-preferred world. Therefore, we need to make sure there are places in every church where every type preference can be experienced.

Type can help church leadership teams work together more effectively. Many church boards study type in order to understand and communicate with each other better. It is often helpful to explore the type of the congregation. Most congregations have a certain feel to them—more intuitive than sensing, for example, or more feeling than thinking. "Typing" the congregation can help the leadership understand what is happening and thus make choices that will help the congregation function in the weaker areas.

All of these issues will be explored in this book. But before we launch into these interesting topics, I would like to give a word of caution.

The Misuse of Type

Now that psychological type is becoming so common, abuses and misuses are becoming common also. The Kiersey-Bates Temperament Sorter, printed in the book *Please Understand Me,*[3] is now available on the World Wide Web. I have heard that a quarter of a million people take it each year. Countless people—in the tens or hundreds of thousands—have participated in Myers-Briggs Type Indicator seminars at work. People have read magazine articles and books to learn about it.

I am concerned that a growing number of people have acquired only a superficial understanding of type. This can lead to problems, some of them serious and others less significant.

One of the less significant problems, but one that saddens me very much, is that so many people tell me they took the Myers-Briggs Type Indicator one time but they can't remember very much about it. Often they can't remember anything at all about it, except that there were some letters involved. I believe it takes about four to six hours to teach the principles of type to a level where there is lasting meaning for the learner. Many people are sitting in seminars where type is taught for a half hour or an hour. It is a complex theory, and I wish people wouldn't teach it at all if they're not going to devote significant time to it.

A superficial understanding of type can lead to a lot of labelling and stereotyping. "My husband is a J and I'm a P. He's neurotic about schedules." Or worse, "My boss is insensitive, so he must be a T." One of the best attributes of Isabel Briggs Myers, the developer of the Myers-Briggs Type Indicator, was her unfailingly positive view of type. Her theme song was the constructive use of differences. All the type descriptions in her book *Gifts Differing*⁴ present healthy, effective human personality patterns. We misuse type when we use it to label unpleasant behavior.

A superficial knowledge of type can lead people to believe that type preferences are a predictor of human behavior. "He can't do that job because of his type." "She's too introverted to fit into those kinds of social situations." "I'm a feeling type, so don't expect me to give logical reasons for my actions." All of us can function in weaker areas when necessary. We must never use personality type to exclude someone from a job or ministry, or to limit our own possibilities. We must never use personality type as an excuse for lack of love or reason.

Type does not lock us into anything. It is a way to describe preferred ways of functioning, but it never tells us that we must function in only that way.

The Limits of the Instruments

The Myers-Briggs Type Indicator has that name for a reason. It is called an indicator because it may indicate a person's type preferences. A certain number of people do not score accurately on the MBTI, if "accurate" means that they later believe, after they understand the principles of type, that their score on the Indicator reflects their true type.

The Kiersey-Bates Temperament Sorter may be even less accurate than the MBTI because it was not statistically validated like the MBTI was.

Each person is the expert on his or her own type. I often wish these tests were not available at all, and that people could sit in a seminar for a whole weekend and learn the principles of type. What is thinking? What is feeling? How would each manifest itself in everyday life? Over the course of the weekend, participants would be able to identify their type based on an understanding of the principles.

Often people say to me, "I score right on the borderline of intuition and sensing. I'm right in the middle."

I respond, "Now that you understand the principles of type, do you have a clearer sense of which one you prefer?"

"Oh, I'm right in the middle."

"Is that based on your understanding of the concepts of intuition and sensing?"

"That's what my test score said, so I must be right in the middle."

Conversations like this make me want to throw away all such instruments! I believe that most people do have at least a fairly clear preference in each of the four preference pairs of psychological type. They may need help to discover their preference. People's test scores are skewed by their mood when taking it, by the values they attach to some of the questions and vocabulary in the tests, and probably by a hundred other factors.

Therefore, when working with people in congregations, we must remember that they may have taken the MBTI in a seminar at work or the Kiersey-Bates Temperament Sorter on the Internet. They may be wedded to their score, but it may not accurately reflect their true preferences. We must be careful to keep people focused on the concepts of type rather than the letters of a score they received.

Despite the potential for stereotyping and despite my frustrations with the tests available to measure type, the principles of psychological type can be immensely helpful in a congregational setting. Type can help us work together more productively to create healthy congregations, and type can help us grow spiritually.

Isabel Briggs Myers stressed that the goal of understanding and using type is to promote the constructive use of differences. In our congregations, as we strive to minister and learn and worship together in this age of incredible diversity, we need help in order to affirm differences while remaining one body. Type is one tool that can help us affirm and understand the differences that God built into people, so that we can work together more effectively. "There are varieties of gifts, but the same Spirit; and there are varieties of services, but the same Lord; and there are varieties of activities, but it is the same God who activates all of them in everyone" (1 Corinthians 12:4-6).

CHAPTER 1

Introduction to Type and Spirituality

In 1923 a remarkable book was translated into English for the first time. A mother and daughter read the book. They started observing the personalities of their family and friends in a new light.

The book was *Psychological Types* by Swiss psychologist Carl Jung.[1] The mother-daughter pair were Katharine Briggs and Isabel Briggs Myers. Katharine Briggs had already developed her own theory of personality type, but she threw it away when she read Jung's because his ideas included her own observations and more.

In 1923 Isabel Myers was a young married woman. She had had an unusual upbringing. Her mother had taught her at home until Isabel went to college. The can-do and can-learn-anything attitude acquired from home schooling was essential in the development of the Myers-Briggs Type Indicator.

During the 1920s and 1930s Katharine and Isabel continued to observe patterns of personality in their family and friends. When World War II began, they were dismayed at the kinds of war work chosen by acquaintances. They believed if people understood their personality better, they would make better choices.

Basing her work on Jung's personality theory, Isabel began to develop a series of questions that would help people identify their personality type. During the next two decades the questions she wrote were checked and re-checked using standards of psychological test validity. The Myers-Briggs Type Indicator was born.

The Indicator was slow to gain acceptance in the community of psychologists because of the fact that Isabel Briggs Myers was not a psychologist. In recent years, however, the MBTI has become the most widely used psychological instrument in the world. Other versions have arisen. The Kiersey-Bates Temperament Sorter is posted on the Internet where some quarter of a million people take it each year.

A children's version, the Murphy-Meisgeier Type Indicator for Children,[2] was developed in the 1980s. A new adult test, the Personality Profiler,[3] was developed in the 1990s. Both of these are validated instruments like the MBTI.

The concepts in the MBTI and the other tests are based mostly on the work of Jung, with a significant addition by Katharine Briggs and Isabel Myers. Jung developed the idea of extraversion and introversion, sensing and intuition, and thinking and feeling. Jung believed that each of us would function in both arenas in each pair, but we would prefer one over the other in each pair.

Katharine and Isabel added the fourth dichotomy of psychological type—judging and perceiving—to indicate whether we prefer taking in information (perceiving) or making decisions about information (judging) when we function in the outer world.

Table 1

THE BASICS OF PERSONALITY TYPE

Attitudes	Source or Direction of Energy	Extraversion	E
		Introversion	I
Functions	Two Ways of Perceiving (Gathering Information)	Sensing	S
		Intuition	N
Functions	Two Ways of Judging (Processing Information)	Thinking	T
		Feeling	F
Attitudes	Orientation to the Outer World	Judging	J
		Perceiving	P

Attitudes: Extraversion and Introversion (E and I)

Jung believed that we function in two different attitudes towards the outer world. When we are energized by the outer world and when our energy is directed toward the outer world, we are using extraversion. The source and focus of our energy is people, things, and activity, all of them external to us.[4]

When we are energized by the inner world of reflection and ideas and when our energy is directed toward our inner world, we are using introversion.[5] All of us use both introversion and extraversion. Most of us prefer one of them over the other. We are more comfortable and less fatigued using the one we prefer. Some of us have extremely strong preferences for one or the other. Others of us have mild preferences. A very small number have no preference at all.

We call extraverts the people who prefer extraversion. Introverts are the people who prefer introversion. In using these terms, we must always remember that extraverts use introversion on occasion. Some extraverts are very competent at focusing on the inner world; they simply don't prefer it as strongly as they prefer extraversion.

In the same way, the people we call introverts can and must function in the outer world. Because we live in a culture that emphasizes physical reality, and because the demands of life by necessity involve some contact with the physical world, it is possible that, on the average, introverts have developed extraverted skills more highly than extraverts have developed introverted skills.

Remember that, according to Jung, the issue is energy. I am an introvert. I prefer introversion over extraversion. When I'm using extraversion, which I do frequently and with some skill, I am much more easily fatigued than when I am using introversion. I am so talkative and friendly that most people think I'm an extravert. However, I can work quietly on a project for hours at a time and be only slightly tired at the end. For me, meetings with large numbers of people or large social events are exhausting after an hour or two.

At midlife most people begin to experience an attraction to developing skills in their least-preferred arenas. Because of this fact and the fact that all extraverts use introversion on occasion and vice versa, it's important not to make global generalizations about what introverts and extraverts will choose to do or not do. At the same time, we can affirm that introversion and extraversion have deep and significant implications in religious communities. We have strong faith values attached to both. The strength of these values varies in different faiths, denominations, and congregations.

As an introverted child, I enjoyed attending the Episcopal worship services of my childhood—until I became a teenager when, of course, no church seemed like a good idea! I remember that as a child I enjoyed entering the sanctuary quietly. The service itself was subdued. There was no passing of the peace in the 1950s and '60s. We went up for communion quietly. At the end of the service everyone left in silence.

All the announcements of congregational events were written in the bulletin. In fact, there were hardly any social events at all. I remember sparsely attended coffee hours and an annual picnic.

It's no wonder to me, looking back, that my very extraverted brother quit attending church as soon as he could and seldom looks back. In fact, I wonder now how any extraverted young adult could find meaning in those extremely quiet churches.

On the other hand, I have visited churches that seem to be designed exclusively for extraverts. So many activities are planned and announced at length that an introvert would feel overwhelmed. The activities— numerous social events and service opportunities that involve large groups of people—sound exhausting to introverts. The passing of the peace or congregational greeting time, usually very difficult for introverts, is so long and effusive that a person feels guilty if he or she hasn't hugged everyone in the congregation. There is not one moment of silence for reflection. Everything happens quickly and loudly.

The center of faith—the issues around the meaning of being a Christian—often varies between introverts and extraverts. Introverts often experience intimacy with God in quiet moments of prayer or reflection. I've often suggested in seminars that introverts long for the day when they would hear from the pulpit, "All church activities have been cancelled for a month so we can all focus on prayer." The introverts in my seminars usually nod vigorously. Many share their deep sadness that the ministry of prayer is not valued in their congregation with the same pleasure and validation as working in the food bank or teaching children.

Extraverts, on the other hand, often find God though serving people or through being together with people. One extraverted woman served her congregation as fellowship elder. With great fondness, she was called "The Party Elder" because she excelled at planning large fellowship events. She met God in those events. She confessed to me once that whenever there was a period of silence in worship or at a retreat, she always felt a deep urge to get up and do something—anything! Usually all she could think of was to go to the bathroom, but doing anything was far better than being forced to sit in silence.

Recent data indicate that about half the population in the United States prefers introversion and half prefers extraversion.[6] Most type watchers believe that, despite this population pattern, our culture values extraversion over introversion. Activity, busy schedules, fast pace, and a huge circle of friends—all these seem to be valued in our culture. My observation is that many churches have bought into our society's values by encouraging extraverted expressions of faith.

Functions: Sensing and Intuition (S and N)

Jung believed that our minds perform two major tasks. We take in information and we make decisions about information. Jung believed we have two ways we take in information and two ways we make decisions about information. The second dichotomy of psychological type—sensing and intuition—describes the two ways we take in information.

When we are taking in information through sensing, we remain in the present reality of the five senses.[7] We notice smells and sounds. We observe a variety of colors. We perceive temperature and humidity. When interacting with people, we take note of body language, posture, tone of voice, facial expression, and other subtle clues.

When we are taking in information through intuition, we remain in the present reality of the senses only long enough to receive enough sensory data to make a leap into the possibilities associated with those data.[8] While sensing focuses on the present and uses memories of the past to provide further information, intuition focuses on the future. Intuition explores the big picture, the overall theme, the patterns that are present, the connections between the pieces of data received, and, above all, the meaning of the information.

Each of us uses both ways of taking in information, but most of us prefer one over the other. People who prefer sensing tend to be practical, factual, and concrete, concerned with the details of each tree rather than studying the forest as a whole. People who prefer intuition tend to be abstract and to think globally. They are concerned with the pattern of the forest rather than the characteristics of the individual trees.

My husband prefers sensing and I prefer intuition. My husband can tell my mood by the set of my shoulders. He notices attractions among the single members of our church by their body language. When we do a house project together, I'm good at keeping track of the big picture—all the tasks that need to be done and in what order—while he is much more meticulous with a paintbrush, hammer, or saw.

When we got married more than 20 years ago, I was leading Bible Study Dig-Ins as an InterVarsity Christian Fellowship staff member. My husband attended many of the Dig-Ins I led, and we assumed that Bible study together—just the two of us—would be a significant part of our marriage. We tried. Really, we tried hard. But my husband is more interested in the details, the repeated words, and the meaning of individual words and sentences. I went crazy, but he also went crazy when I wanted to discuss overall themes and larger patterns. He thought I didn't spend enough time gathering data upon which to build the themes. I wanted to jump as soon as possible to the questions of meaning and purpose. I thought he spent far too much time on the details, which bored me.

This difference is also visible when reading financial reports. I have observed that people who prefer sensing cannot read the bottom line until they have read sequentially through all the other lines, while people who prefer intuition cannot read all the lines of detail until they have grasped the bottom line. Intuitives often become rapidly bored with too much detail. Sensing types often do not understand why intuitives have to keep asking "why?" instead of sticking with the facts, which are so much easier to agree about.

Sensing and intuition are the hardest to observe of the four psychological type dichotomies. Because information is absorbed inside our minds, these functions tend to be somewhat invisible. Even if they are hard to observe, they have profound implications for the way we function together in a congregation.

Sensing types, because they are usually oriented to the present and the past, often have a high regard for tradition and a profound respect for institutional memory and the record-keeping required to maintain our connection to our past. They often excel at the kind of gestures that

communicate appreciation and thanks to volunteers. The physical surroundings in their house of worship may be quite important to sensing
types.

Intuitives, with their orientation to future possibilities and overarching themes, are likely to be concerned with questions of meaning and
purpose. Are we being faithful to the call of God? Are we remembering
what is most important about faith? Intuitives make a great contribution
to a church community by helping everyone to remember these larger
questions. At the same time, intuitives can become bored with the mun-
dane details involved in running a church, such as record-keeping and
building maintenance.

Some significant differences of opinion in churches can arise from
this sensing-intuition dichotomy. Consultants Otto Kroeger and Roy
Oswald conducted research for the Alban Institute showing that 57 percent of American Protestant clergy prefer intuition, while 76 percent of
the United States population prefers sensing.[9] Congregations vary in
their proportion of sensing and intuitive types, and certainly some congregations have a majority of members who prefer intuition, but probably most congregations in the United States have a majority of members who prefer sensing. An intuitive pastor and a predominantly sensing
congregation can bless each other greatly. They can also irritate each
other profoundly.

In personal spirituality, sensing and intuition can look quite different also. When we use sensing in connecting with God, we find God in
and through the gifts of our five senses and through memory. When we
meet God through intuition, we are more attracted to images and metaphors. We all use both of these patterns of spirituality, but we usually
prefer one over the other.

Functions: Thinking and Feeling (T and F)

Carl Jung called sensing and intuition "functions" because they are two
ways that our brains function to take in information. Jung also observed
two ways that our minds function to make decisions about information—
thinking and feeling.

The choice of words in English is unfortunate because in the 1990s
there are so many values associated with the word "feeling," such as the

commonly held desire to "get in touch with our feelings" and the identi-
fication of the word feeling with personal passions. In addition, there is
still residue from the past that equates expressing feelings with being
emotional, feminine, and illogical.

Jung's use of the word feeling has very little connection to our
culture's use of the word. He is contrasting two ways of making decisions. When he uses the word feeling, he is referring to a decisionmaking
pattern that involves concern for human values and that strives primarily
for relational harmony. It is decisionmaking based on deeply held values.
In contrast, the word "thinking" involves making decisions with a
concern for logic and truth. Thinking is more detached and objective
than feeling.[10]

Both processes involve what our culture might call thinking and
feeling. Both processes involve processing information, what we might
call "thinking it over." Both can involve exploring what we feel emo-
tionally about the question at hand. Therefore, when we are discussing
psychological type, we have to be very careful to remember that the
technical terms "thinking" and "feeling," as used to describe type, involve specific ways of making judgments about information we have
received. Thinking involves a concern for logic and truth; feeling involves a concern for values and harmony.

When we use thinking, we are usually able to articulate fairly pre-
cisely the thought processes that brought us to our decision. We usually
have reasons. We are usually concerned with issues of right and wrong,
and we often feel connected to some kind of objective truth.

When we use feeling, we often simply know that a decision is the
right one. We may find it difficult to describe the process that got us to
the decision, but we are sure that the people involved will be best served
by this particular decision. When we use feeling, we are most connected
to issues of harmony and people-values.

I was raised in a family of thinkers, and I too prefer thinking. I always believed that if people couldn't articulate a reason why they had
made a decision, then they were likely to be wrong. I also believed that
if there were two opposing decisions being discussed, the one that had
more logical reasons attached to it was more likely to be right.

I have come to understand and appreciate the feeling decisionmaking
process. I may have a hundred reasons why I believe my decision is best,
but I could be wrong. Logical analysis alone doesn't guarantee accuracy.

When our decisions involve human beings, there are so many issues under the surface. Someone using a feeling preference in making a decision is just as likely to get it right as I am, even if I can articulate my logic more clearly.

Thinking and feeling are the only psychological type dichotomies that are gender-linked. Roughly two-thirds of men prefer thinking and about two-thirds of women prefer feeling. Our culture has traditionally put a high value on thinking, but the situation may be changing. Many observers have noted a kind of paradigm shift in the corporate and scientific worlds with changes brought about by globalization and new ways of considering the world, including the theory of relativity, systems theory, and chaos theory. All of these affirm the interrelatedness of the created order which has a stronger connection to feeling than the older patterns of thought which are more detached, linear, and logic-based.

In some religious settings thinking is valued highly, with emphasis on theology, order and discipline, and structure. In other settings feeling is valued highly, with the accent on caring ministries, empowering people, and teamwork. In some ways the thinking-feeling dichotomy captures the enigma of Jesus being full of both grace and truth. Jesus came to fulfill the law, not abolish it, and he spoke uncompromising truth in many diverse settings. Yet he communicated grace through his actions and words, with deep concern for human harmony.

In congregations the thinking-feeling preference may be the most explosive and painful aspect of psychological type differences. It can be difficult for people who prefer thinking and feeling to respect each other. The feeling type proposes an action. The thinking type asks, "Why?" The feeling type thinks, "If she really respected me, she wouldn't need to hear reasons." The thinking type, meanwhile, is wondering, "If he can't articulate his reasons, can this really be a good idea?"

People who prefer thinking are more likely to be comfortable with procedures and policies, while people who prefer feeling are more likely to want to make each decision afresh, with consideration for specific people and particular circumstances. When the thinking types propose policies, the feeling types can perceive the policies as narrow and too limiting. The thinking types can become frustrated with the feeling commitment to take so many circumstances into consideration in making decisions. It can feel too slow and cumbersome.

Yet, at its best, teamwork in the area of thinking and feeling can be wonderfully effective. The thinking types provide enough order and structure for the feeling types to relax, and the feeling types continually bring the needs of people into the forefront so that the thinking types don't need to worry that people are being overlooked.

Two More Attitudes: Judging and Perceiving (J and P)

The three dichotomies presented above are the work of Carl Jung. The final pair of dichotomies in psychological type—judging and perceiving—are the brain child of Isabel Briggs Myers and Katharine Briggs.

Jung laid out the attitudes toward the outer world: extraversion and introversion. Then he proposed that there are two major tasks of the mind: taking in information (perceiving) and making decisions about information (judging). He believed that there are two ways of perceiving (sensing and intuition) and two ways of judging (thinking and feeling).

As Briggs and Myers studied Jung's theory of psychological type, they came to believe that each of us has a preferred way of functioning in the outer world. Some of us live our outward lives most comfortably taking in information, or perceiving. Some of us are more comfortable living outwardly in the realm of making decisions or judgments rather than always taking in more information.[11]

Thus, in psychological type, perceiving refers to a preference for keeping things open, for continuing to retain in a perceptive attitude. People who prefer perceiving often come across as flexible and easygoing.

Judging refers to a preference for making decisions over taking in more information. People who prefer judging often seem to be organized, structured, committed to deadlines, and aware of schedules.

Judging and perceiving refer to our preferences in the outer world. Briggs and Myers believed that most people would use one function in the outer world and the other in the inner world. For example, I have preferences for intuition, thinking, and judging. My preference for judging means that I will use my judging function (thinking) in the outer world, while in the inner world I will use my perceiving function (intuition).

Briggs and Myers devised the fourth pair of preferences to help us understand the relative importance of each of the functions we use. This judging-perceiving preference results in observable patterns of behavior.

In churches these two preferences have great impact on the decision-making process. People who prefer judging are often more ready to make decisions. Sometimes they neglect to consider all the necessary information, and they often don't allow for some kind of process to continue to take in necessary information even after the decision is made.

People who prefer perceiving are often slower to make decisions, sometimes too slow from the point of view of those who prefer judging. In this day of information overload, the challenge for the perceiver is to know when to stop the flow of information and make a decision.

As a person who prefers judging, I am most comfortable working with others who prefer judging, because together we can be organized and decisive at a comfortable pace. I have learned, though, that I need to work with people who prefer perceiving; otherwise, important data and options are neglected. My drive to move toward a decision needs to be moderated by those who have a better sense of all the information that needs to be considered.

God

Bruce Duncan, an Anglican minister and director of a retreat center in Salisbury, England, has a wonderful section in his book *Pray Your Way*[12] about the ways that these personality characteristics come from God.

"Your ability to extravert is a gift from God," he writes. "The God who delights to pour love, creative energy, outwards to form and hold in existence the material universe is an extravert God. . . . You can glimpse the mystery of God through the created universe."[13] We meet the extravert God in scientific discoveries about the creation, in the wonder of the animal kingdom, and as we connect with other people in fellowship and worship.

Duncan continues to say that we can see in God the gift of introversion. "Whenever you introvert, you focus your life energy within yourself. The energy of God's life and love is discovered within the divine mystery of the Holy Trinity, Creator and Redeemer united in love by the Holy Spirit. . . . The interior life of God is utterly beyond our comprehension, rich beyond our imagining and the source of our own ability to introvert."[14]

God is a sensing God, Duncan continues, "the God of all that is real to the senses, the macro to the micro, from the galaxies to the minutest particle of matter. God joyfully creates the sun and the moon, the snowflake and the stork, the Korean hanging bellied pig and the dolphin, and delights to share his sensing gift with his creatures."[15] The present-oriented time focus of the sensing type mirrors God as eternally present.

God is also an intuitive God. "Who imagined the imaginable? Who dreamed up the created universe? The visionary intuitive God is never afraid to take risks, perceiving eternally new patterns and possibilities, always finding the creative way through any problem. God is the mysterious and hidden God, revealed in symbol, allusion and paradox."[16] Intuition allows us to connect with the God of the future, the God of purpose and plan.

Whenever we use the thinking gift of logical, rational judgment, we "reflect the nature of a God who is righteous, faithful, and true." Our "ability to be objective, to take a long cool look at the evidence and judge accordingly, derives from the Thinking God who is infinitely just and totally impartial." We can argue with God, "who is consistent, never fickle or unreasonable. In fact, our very insistence that God should be God, and display a passionate justice, is in itself a reflection in us of the Thinking image of God."[17] Duncan believes that when we bring our honest doubts and questions to God, we are reflecting the thinking image of God in us.

The feeling God enters into our sorrows and suffering and feels the world's pain. In addition, "The feeling God is the great encourager, who longs for us to live in harmony with one another."[18] Duncan cites the New Testament emphasis on peace as an evidence of this feeling aspect of God's character, which has nothing to do with being swayed by emotion, but is related to goodness, loyalty, tenderness, and mercy.

When we use our judging attitude and desire closure, decisiveness, structure, and order, we reflect the image of the judging God. Duncan points out that God is not fickle, but is a God who "judges, decides, chooses, calls, acts." This God lays before us choices and decisions. "Stability, order, reliability, discernment, sound judgment, trustworthiness are human virtues that reflect the J God."[19]

Whenever we adopt the perceiving attitude, we are reflecting the "image of the One who is infinitely open, receptive and spontaneous. . . . God's judgment is never hasty. He is always 'slow to anger.' The inquiring, open-minded P attitude in human personality images the God who listens, observes, and waits patiently for us." When we are being "open to whatever life offers, curious, spontaneous, fun-loving, [we] are reflecting the ebullient God of delight and joy, who laughs and plays and enjoys creation, the Perceiving God in whom there is an endless Sabbath rest."[20]

Certainly God is more than these eight attributes, and we reflect the image of God in more than eight ways. It is still enjoyable, encouraging, and challenging to consider the ways the eight personality-type preferences mirror aspects of God's character.

Considering Type Patterns

Once we have clarified each of our preferences, we can then begin to look for patterns in the ways our preferences work together. The four preference letters combine together into 16 possible types.

Many type teachers find it useful to divide the 16 types into other groupings. One common way to teach and learn about type is to consider the four function pairs: ST, SF, NT, and NF. Several books on type and spirituality explore type using these groupings. Lutheran minister and type consultant Gary Harbaugh, in *God's Gifted People*, assigns very helpful descriptors to each of the four function pairs:

> ST - The Gift of Practicality: Living in the Here and Now
> SF - The Gift of Personal Helpfulness: Reaching Out and Lifting Up
> NF - The Gift of Possibilities for People: Keeping Hope Alive
> NT - The Gift of Looking Ahead: Letting the Future Guide the Present[21]

Harbaugh also presents common patterns of service for each of the four function pairs.

In *Four Spiritualities* Peter T. Richardson, who made a lifelong study of world religions, sets out to explore the religions of the world using the lens of type. He describes four spiritual patterns or pathways based on the function pairs, and draws on literature from many religions of the world to illustrate these four pathways. Again, his names for the pathways are useful to consider:

ST - Journey of Works
SF - Journey of Devotion
NF - Journey of Harmony
NT - Journey of Unity.[22]

Another way of dividing the 16 types into four groups is the temperament types developed by David Kiersey and Marilyn Bates, who are psychologists and trainers of therapists. Kiersey and Bates use the four temperaments of Hippocrates—sanguine, choleric, phlegmatic, and melancholic—and present four patterns of behavior based on type that mirror these four temperaments. Their temperament types are SP, SJ, NT, and NF.[23] This way of breaking the 16 types into four groupings is common in business consulting settings, but only one book has been written linking spirituality with these temperament types. It is *Prayer and Temperament* by Catholic writers Chester P. Michael and Marie C. Norrisey.[24] Using the function pairs, rather than temperament types, seems to access a structure that is more relevant to spiritual issues.

There is one reason to consider the temperament types and church issues. It comes from unpublished research by Otto Kroeger and Roy Oswald. They studied the patterns of church attendance in the United States and found that the more liberal the congregation, the higher the percentage of intuitives. On the other end of the spectrum, more conservative congregations had a higher percentage of SJs. Missing almost entirely from the North American church scene were SPs. Otto Kroeger, a Lutheran pastor and popular author and consultant on personality type, believes that the church needs seriously to address ministry to this segment of the population that is largely absent from congregations.

Many other authors discuss spirituality and type using the four functions themselves: sensing, intuition, feeling, and thinking. Bruce Duncan presents patterns of prayer based on each of the four functions.[25] Roman Catholic writers Clarke, Thompson, and Grant in *From Image to Likeness* present patterns of spirituality based on each of the four functions:

A Gift to be Simple (Sensing/Simplicity)
The Truth That Makes Us Free (Thinking/Justice)
With a Joyful Heart (Feeling/Gratitude)
Eye Has Not Seen (Intuiting/Hope)[26]

Table 2

PATTERNS WITHIN TYPE
(used by different authors to discuss type and spirituality)

Function Pairs	ST
	SF
	NT
	NF
Temperament Types	SJ
	SP
	NT
	NF
Functions	S
	N
	T
	F
Functions with Attitudes	ES
	IS
	EN
	IN
	ET
	IT
	EF
	IF

Dominant Functions

The functions are the middle two letters of one's type. There are four
functions and we each prefer two of them. Of these four functions—
sensing, intuition, thinking, and feeling—one of them is used most often
by each of us. We call this most-used function the dominant function.
One function is used second-most, and we call it the auxiliary function.
The dominant and auxiliary functions appear in our types as the middle
two letters.

  We also use the functions that do not appear in our type. These two
functions are our tertiary (third) and inferior (fourth) functions. Table 3
on page 17 lists the dominant, auxiliary, tertiary, and inferior functions
for each type.

  We use the last letter of our type, J or P, combined with our preference for introversion or extraversion, to determine our dominant function.

  The letter at the end of our type (J or P) tells us which function we
use in the outer world. Let's consider Sandra, ESFP. The P tells us that
in the outer world she prefers to remain in a perceiving attitude. There
are two perceiving functions—sensing and intuition. Of those two,
Sandra prefers sensing. Therefore, the function she uses most frequently
in the outer world is sensing. Because it is used in the outer world, we
call it extraverted sensing.

Table 3

CHART OF FUNCTIONS

	Dominant #1	Auxiliary #2	Tertiary* #3	Inferior #4
ISTJ	S (I)	T (E)	F	N (E)
ISFJ	S (I)	F (E)	T	N (E)
INFJ	N (I)	F (E)	T	S (E)
INTJ	N (I)	T (E)	F	S (E)
ISTP	T (I)	S (E)	N	F (E)
ISFP	F (I)	S (E)	N	T (E)
INFP	F (I)	N (E)	S	T (E)
INTP	T (I)	N (E)	S	F (E)
ESTP	S (E)	T (I)	F	N (I)
ESFP	S (E)	F (I)	T	N (I)
ENFP	N (E)	F (I)	T	S (I)
ENTP	N (E)	T (I)	F	S (I)
ESTJ	T (E)	S (I)	N	F (I)
ESFJ	F (E)	S (I)	N	T (I)
ENFJ	F (E)	N (I)	S	T (I)
ENTJ	T (E)	N (I)	S	F (I)

*The dominant function is used in the preferred attitude (extraversion or intraversion.) The auxiliary and inferior (the second and fourth) functions are used in the opposite attitude from the dominant function. There is disagreement about the attitude of the third, or tertiary function. It is left blank on this chart because it seems to vary with the individual.

Sandra uses her judging function in her inner world. There are two judging functions—thinking and feeling. Of those two, she prefers feeling. Therefore Sandra most frequently uses feeling in the inner world of thoughts and ideas. Because feeling is used inwardly, we call it introverted feeling.

So Sandra has two functions that she uses most often: extraverted sensing and introverted feeling. She uses one of these two functions more often. Because of her preference for extraversion, it is the extraverted function—extraverted sensing—that she uses more often. We call extraverted sensing her dominant function. She will use introverted feeling second-most often. We call introverted feeling her auxiliary function.

The situation is slightly different for introverts. Let's consider Josh, INFJ. The J tells us that he uses a judging function in the outer world. The judging function that he prefers is feeling. Because it is used in the outer world, it is extraverted feeling.

He uses the other function, the perceiving function, in the inner world. His preferred perceiving function is intuition. Because it is used in the inner world, it is introverted intuition.

So Josh has two functions he uses most often: extraverted feeling and introverted intuition. Because he is an introvert, his preferred function of these two is introverted intuition. It is his dominant function. Extraverted feeling is his auxiliary. Josh's dominant function will be virtually invisible because it is used inside. People are able to observe extraverted feeling—Josh's warmth and gentle caring—but they won't see his introverted intuition very easily. This is the irony of introversion, that our most preferred function can barely be experienced by the people around us.

The dominant function is important because we develop it first in life and because we use it most often. In fact, we could say that the long-term goal of type development is to become so competent in our use of our dominant function that it is informed by all the other functions.

The dominant function is also important because its opposite is our least-used function—the inferior function or the least-preferred function. The inferior function has great impact on our life of faith, particularly after midlife. We will explore the inferior function as it relates to prayer in chapter 4 and as it relates to growth in faith in chapter 5.

In the rest of this book we will explore many other issues related to the preferences described in this chapter. Leadership patterns, conflict, scheduling and planning church events, pastoral care, service opportunities . . . all of these are influenced by our type preferences, and type can help us work together better in our congregations.

CHAPTER 2

Using Type to Find a Place to Serve

Rebecca is a Christian who recently moved to a new town. She visits several churches and finally settles on one. She wants to get involved and make friends. She also wants to find a place to make a contribution in the church. She decides to help in a Sunday school classroom, and she volunteers to tutor neighborhood children in the congregation's tutoring program. Within a few months Rebecca has begun to get to know the people with whom she volunteers. She enjoys working with children in both Sunday school and the tutoring program, and she feels a sense of contribution to her church. She is becoming part of a community.

Joan and Dale begin attending the same church at the same time. Dale, quite reserved, finds it difficult to be enthusiastic about any of the ministries he hears about on Sunday mornings. Joan makes a concerted effort to find a place to belong in the church. Like Rebecca, she volunteers to work with children once a month, but the frustrations outweigh any satisfaction she experiences in the nursery. The schedule is poorly administered. She is a person who likes to plan ahead, but she receives several calls at the last minute on Sunday mornings asking her to work in the nursery. One Sunday morning Joan is left in the nursery with five toddlers without any other adults present. She knows the church has a policy that at least two adults must be with a group of children at all times, so she feels very uneasy that morning. She decides to quit working in the nursery and she never finds another place that feels comfortable. Joan and Dale continue to attend worship for a while, but eventually they drift away from the church.

Rebecca, Joan, and Dale—like many new folks in congregations, along with some long-time members—are looking for ways to be useful in their church. They want to make a contribution. They want to serve because they know that Christ calls us to service. They hope to find a place where they can feel they are making a meaningful contribution in the congregation or in its ministry to the larger world. They understand that they will draw nearer to God as they serve. And they desire to experience satisfaction and meaning in their church service, perhaps in contrast to their work.

Accompanying this desire to feel useful is the longing to belong, to experience community. Many new church attenders feel that if they could find a place to serve, they would meet congenial people who would become like extended family, providing connection and support. They're right. Serving together is an excellent way to get to know people and make long-lasting friendships. Serving together helps us feel connected.

Unfortunately, many newcomers never find a place to serve, and many long-time members burn out in their places of service. Personality type can be a helpful tool when exploring issues around service, but there are limits to what type can do. When we understand these limits, we can use type appropriately to help people as they seek to find a place to serve.

Elizabeth's Story

Elizabeth is an organized, energetic, detail-oriented woman in her seventies. Whenever she takes spiritual gifts inventories, she scores highest in service and administration. Her type preferences are ESTJ.

Elizabeth is an Episcopalian. She has always enjoyed serving on the altar guild in the various churches she attended with her family. She is highly skilled at ironing the exquisite altar cloths, and she enjoys keeping things tidy. This ministry, constant throughout most of Elizabeth's adult life, makes a lot of sense when you consider her ESTJ preferences.

When Elizabeth's kids reached high school, Elizabeth got involved in two other ministries that have continued for more than 25 years. First, she began serving on the board of a celebrity lecture series that raises money for charity. Over the years, she has been involved in all kinds of planning and implementation that draw on her ESTJ strengths. In addition, she greatly enjoys picking up the celebrity lecturers at the airport.

She helps them deal with their luggage, takes them to their hotel, and makes sure they are settled in comfortably. She draws on the strengths that make her an excellent hostess in her own home. She is gregarious, friendly, and very practical. All these strengths fit beautifully with the ESTJ profile.

Elizabeth has also been involved in hospice for more than 20 years, and this ministry is less easy to match with her Myers-Briggs type. Yet hospice has been a significant source of growth and personal development for her.

When Elizabeth first heard about volunteering with hospice, she thought that she would go into the home of a dying patient and help the caregiver in practical ways. Maybe she would wash dishes or do laundry or buy groceries. These practical tasks appealed to her because she loves to be helpful in this way.

Instead, she found that most caregivers need to get out of the house. Volunteering with hospice, she discovered, usually means sitting with the dying patient while the caregiver runs errands or gets a haircut. Volunteering involves lots of listening to the patient and especially to the caregiver. Hospice ministry is a ministry of presence, coming alongside without giving advice, listening without a lot of comment. If we were to pick the ideal psychological type to do this kind of ministry, we might pick INFP, the exact opposite of Elizabeth.

In the first 15 years of her service with hospice, Elizabeth fell into a pattern. She would volunteer in people's homes once or twice a week for a year or two, maybe working with two or three dying patients consecutively. Then she would take a turn on the hospice board where she could use her abundant energy for administrative tasks. She might organize fund-raising events or act as a liaison with a hospital board.

As so often happens, about ten years ago the hospice organization in her town was absorbed into a hospital which was later bought by another medical company. At each step there have been more boards related to hospice. A foundation was established. In recent years, Elizabeth has served exclusively on different boards.

Throughout the 20-plus years in hospice, Elizabeth has grown immensely in understanding how to care for people in pain. She has developed listening skills.

Elizabeth says, "I'm not a quiet person! Through hospice I've learned some of the many things you can do to help people talk. When you're mourning, you need to talk and cry, not keep it in. I've learned how to develop a silent bond with people, and I developed a silent bond with God. So often I would sit praying for the person. Also, I would have to pray that God would help me keep quiet when they talked." Elizabeth says she often received guidance from God as to what to say or ask next.

Hospice has been very meaningful and stretching for Elizabeth. She has deepened in faith. She has been involved in something she really believes in. She has learned valuable skills.

When Elizabeth reflects on her early years with hospice, she realizes that serving with hospice forced her to rely on God more. During those same years, she became more involved in the leadership of her church. She says, "Hospice put me in a position to need God more, and at the same time I became more active at church, which gave me more of God."

Type and Direction for Service

Let's step back to the time when Elizabeth's kids started high school and she was open to stepping into new areas of service. Let's suppose that you were the pastor of Elizabeth's church, and she came to you for advice. You decided to give her the Myers-Briggs Type Indicator to help her explore new directions to serve. Based on her type, ESTJ, would you have suggested that she try hospice? Probably not.

Psychological type is not a good source of direction for finding a place to serve. Type can provide us great understanding of how to serve once we get to a place of ministry. Type can help us understand what tasks will be easy and what tasks will be hard. Type can help us understand which tasks will be tiring. Type can help us predict some of the ways we may experience conflict with people.

The best and most effective service grows out of our deeply held values, commitments, and passions, which give us energy to persevere when things become boring or difficult. These values, commitments, and passions can come from a variety of places in our lives.

In Elizabeth's case her commitment to hospice came from an event in her childhood. Elizabeth had three brothers, and when she was 11, a sister was born. Elizabeth's mother was extremely busy with farm work, so Elizabeth took care of her little sister for many hours each day. When

Elizabeth's sister was 14 months old, she died of a febrile seizure. In those depression years no one seemed to understand how deeply children grieve, and no one in Elizabeth's family had the skills to talk with her about how she felt.

Her grief sat there, deep inside, until she was able to resolve it by serving with hospice. All the hospice seminars she attended on mourning and all the skills she learned about how to listen were part of her healing. A significant part of Elizabeth's growth in faith through hospice came through the healing of her own grief. No one administering the MBTI to Elizabeth could have known about this part of her past or about the power to persevere that it would give her.

Many of the books on spiritual gifts and many books on type imply that if we understand our spiritual gifts and/or our type, they will guide us into a place of meaningful service. Elizabeth's story illustrates a different view. Our passions, our commitments, and our values, which grow out of our life experience, guide us to a place of service. Once we get to that place, our spiritual gifts and our type can help us figure out how to serve.

Elizabeth's service with the altar guild and her involvement with the lecture series provide a comfortable balance for each other. The altar guild uses her ES ability to be in touch with the physical world and her gift of service. The lecture series draws on her TJ organizational gifts and her extraverted love of people and action. Either one would probably become unsatisfying if she spent many hours every week there, because both draw almost entirely on her strengths and give her little opportunity to develop in her weaker areas.

The decision to serve with hospice grew out of her deep concern that people who grieve need support. When she volunteers in people's homes, she is working out of her less developed area, but the training on listening skills provided by the hospice organization has helped her grow and develop in that area. When she serves on one of the boards, she is able to use her strengths. This balance—the ability to grow in a weak area and also use her strengths—is the key to why her hospice service has been so satisfying to her.

Pitfalls When Teaching Type and Spiritual Gifts

We can easily do a disservice to the members of our congregations when we teach them about type and spiritual gifts. There are two common pitfalls.

The first common error is teaching that personality type and spiritual gifts alone will lead us toward satisfying service opportunities. In some cases that's true, but more often finding a place to serve requires that we consider many factors. Some of the questions that should be considered are:

- Who and what do I really care about? For what age groups, what programs, what aspects of congregational life, what ministries in my community, what population groups do I feel the strongest emotions?
- What motivates me? When I talk, what subjects energize me?
- What tasks have I enjoyed in the past?
- What experiences have shaped me?

A second common error is to teach that we will be the most satisfied and that we will make the greatest contribution serving in ministries where we can use our strengths most of the time. This viewpoint considers involvement in ministry almost like an equation: In ministry A I'll be able to use my strengths 80 percent of the time, and in ministry B I'll use my strengths 60 percent of the time, therefore I should choose ministry A.

It is far more important to consider which skills will be used during the 20 to 40 percent (or more!) of the time when one's strengths will not be employed. Do those tasks, the more difficult ones, complement what I do at work? Do they help me grow in new areas? Do they sound like an interesting challenge? Or like a horrible burden?

Perhaps ministry B is a much better choice, with more balance and more positive challenge. Type can help us discern the kind of challenge involved.

Twenty years ago, if Elizabeth had understood type, she could have said, "No wonder I get tired when I serve as a volunteer in people's homes. I have to use my feeling function. Because it's my inferior function, I'm not very good at it, so it involves a lot of effort to use it. But it's satisfying, too, to experience growth there. In my childhood I longed for someone with a well-developed feeling function to listen to my pain about my sister's death. Now I'm able to help others in that way. It's draining for me, but challenging and satisfying at the same time."

Finding a Place to Serve

Type can help us understand the joys and difficulties of a particular kind of service. Type can also help us make wise choices as we find a place to serve. Here are several stories that illustrate the kinds of insights we can find in understanding type.

John, an ISFJ who works for a software company, used to volunteer at church helping with the computers. He found that his volunteer service too closely paralleled his job, so he burned out quickly.

A couple of years later John volunteered to serve as church bookkeeper. In his first months as bookkeeper, he changed many of the ways the money is tracked in the church. He enjoyed the challenge of brainstorming solutions to complex problems. These problems presented him with the opportunity to use his intuition, his inferior function. Some of his enjoyment as bookkeeper probably came from the opportunity to be stretched while still using his ISFJ commitment to precision and organization of detail.

We'll see in the next chapter that burnout can often be prevented by having a balance in our ministries and including some tasks that draw on our weakest areas.

I met Janine and Sandra in one of the first classes on type I taught in a church. I was delighted to find that they were both INTJs like I am. I love to meet other INTJs and find out where they enjoy serving in churches.

Both Janine and Sandra were involved in their church's theater ministry, and both of them clearly had a passion for theater. Janine functioned as an administrator for the church's theater program. She said she loved being organized, tracking details, and keeping things running smoothly. She occasionally directed plays, but she much preferred to function behind the scenes, arranging publicity, overseeing costumes and sets, or figuring out finances. Janine came across as cool and competent.

Sandra, on the other hand, seemed passionate and fiery. She often starred in the church plays, and she preferred to act even in a small role rather than to serve behind the scenes. She was deeply concerned about right and wrong, and she loved to act in plays that communicated an important piece of truth.

At the time, I was involved in my church as an adult education teacher. I enjoy attending plays, but I have absolutely no desire to be involved in producing them or in acting.

We were three women, all the same type, but with very different ministries. Yet there were common threads. I could identify with Sandra's passion for truth. That's at the foundation of why I like to teach adult classes. And I could relate to Janine's passion for having things run smoothly. I get very frustrated when things are disorganized. I often end up running something because I can't bear to have it be sloppy.

These common threads come from our type. Our TJ preference, which we use in the outer world, can manifest itself in a concern for organization or a concern for truth. Interestingly, when Sandra, Janine, and I started talking about our prayer lives, we found even more in common. We all seemed to have a deeply satisfying pattern of private prayer based on our dominant function—introverted intuition. When we talked about prayer, which occurs more in the introverted realm (our preferred arena), the three of us were definitely "talking the same language."

I don't know where Janine's and Sandra's passion for theater came from, but it was wonderful that their church had a ministry where they could exercise that passion. And it was wonderful that they had both found places in the theater ministry where they could be themselves, use their strengths, and experience joy.

Janine's, Sandra's, and my choices for ministry setting clearly illustrate that different types will be involved in very different ministries. There will be common threads in what people enjoy and struggle with, and there will be great differences due to background, passions, and interests.

Mark and Ron both have the same type preferences, ISTJ. Mark is deeply involved in the men's ministry at his church. He loves to organize retreats. Ron, on the other hand, has never once attended a men's retreat.

Mark was raised in a family that participated enthusiastically in church activities. Some of his best memories come from church family retreats he attended with his family as a child. The setting, a wooded retreat center in the mountains, provided a marvelous contrast to the urban surroundings at home. He remembers one retreat when he was ten or 11 when he found an enormous anthill and spent part of an afternoon watching it with his friends. All these wonderful memories fuel his passion for getting men away from the city and out into the woods to talk about God. He uses his ISTJ organizational abilities to plan and organize retreats, with joy and enthusiasm.

Ron, on the other hand, has no positive memories about retreats. In high school he participated in Young Life retreats a few times and found them extremely difficult. He remembers one time when the Young Life staff kept all the kids up until 3:00 A.M. doing line dances. Ron was often sick as a child, and he knew he wasn't feeling well that evening, but the counselors wouldn't let him go to bed. He got so sick after that weekend that he missed eight days of school, including an important tennis tournament. His impression of retreats is a flurry of extraverted activity, no place for individuality, and too many people. He obviously would not be the person to ask to head up the next men's retreat! He needs to find somewhere else to serve, someplace that draws on his enthusiasm and energy.

Mark's and Ron's stories may seem obvious, but we are often tempted to believe that because one ISTJ enjoys a certain ministry, then all other ISTJs ought to consider participating in that same ministry. If Mark and Ron were learning about type and service at the same seminar, everyone might wonder why Ron doesn't want to do what Mark so obviously enjoys doing.

A much more effective use of type would be to consider the kinds of people that Mark, who excels at planning and organizing, needs to draw into leadership with him in order to lead an effective retreat. Who will warmly welcome the men who attend (feeling)? Who will consider questions of meaning: why are we having this retreat and how will we communicate that purpose to the congregation (intuition and feeling)? Who will address individual needs in terms of creature comforts (sensing and feeling)? Who will be sure the teaching is clear, challenging, and life transforming (intuition and thinking)?

There is no reason Mark can't tackle some of these issues because, as we've said, our type doesn't limit us to service in only our areas of strength. But it is unrealistic to think that he will have the energy to tackle all of them, because they are all weaker areas for him.

Serving in Congregations versus Activity at Work

John, mentioned above, found that he needs to serve at church doing something different from what he does at work. Rhonda feels the same way.

Rhonda, ENFJ, works for the city. She organizes programs for children and parents. She is deeply committed to the welfare of people in need and she is a competent administrator. She is capable of juggling many ideas and programs.

She wants to do something different at church. She was asked to serve as the church's elder for adult Christian education. For many years she had served on the Adult Christian Education Committee. She is committed to helping adults learn and grow in faith, and she loves to attend adult classes. But she knew that running the program requires the same kind of administrative skills that she uses at work. She pretty much uses up those skills in her work life, she decided.

Rhonda agreed instead to take on the role of elder for small groups. The church has quite a few small groups, but no organized program to encourage the development of new groups or to support existing groups. Rhonda has a passion for community, and she loves to ponder how to nurture and develop community.

Her passion for community, like her passion for children and parents, is understandable because of her dominant function, extraverted feeling. Her role at church gives her the opportunity to develop her auxiliary function, introverted intuition. She has done lots of thinking about community since taking on the role of elder in the area of small groups. She's been asking questions: Where else in the congregation do people experience community besides small groups? How can those opportunities be better promoted? What helps small groups function effectively? In what ways can the congregation better support small groups?

All these questions draw on her intuition—seeing the big picture, making connections, exploring possibilities. Rhonda made a wise choice to pick an area of service that draws on her strengths but in a different way than her job does.

Serving at Midlife

At midlife and beyond, people usually grow in their ability to use their less-preferred functions. In *Navigating Midlife* the authors write that beginning at midlife, people "need to expand their identity by looking inward to discover the pieces of their personalities that are not yet developed. They need to move toward their own wholeness."[1] The push to grow toward wholeness often motivates people to try new areas of service that they never before would have considered.

This common pattern of developing less-preferred functions at midlife can often be recognized long afterwards. Most people don't consciously choose to develop weak areas; they simply get involved in new areas because that's where their interests lead them.

For many people the midlife years are a wonderful time of integration in which we begin to see the diverse threads of our lives knit together in God's service. Midlife can embolden church members to try new avenues of service. Because all of their functions are now working together more effectively, people at this stage often find new competence in ministry areas that were previously very difficult for them.

At midlife an ISTJ might get involved in Stephen Ministry, an interdenominational program teaching listening skills, and enjoy using intuition and feeling in listening to people in pain. An ENFP may experiment with contemplative prayer, finding particular satisfaction in using introverted sensing and introverted thinking in meditation on a biblical text. An INFJ may take on a concrete task like organizing the ushers or caring for the congregation's garden, finding satisfaction in the sensing and thinking aspects of these responsibilities.

Let's look again at Elizabeth, whose motivation for serving with hospice came from her long-held pain over her sister's death. Elizabeth was in her 40s when she began to volunteer with hospice. She signed up because she thought she would be able to use her practical caring skills, but it turned out that what this type of service required most was in her less preferred areas. The very skills she needed, the INFP skills of coming alongside and caring without giving advice and without needing something specific to happen, were deep inside her, undeveloped and not often used. Because she was in her 40s and 50s and was developing in previously unexplored areas, it makes sense that she would persevere in a setting that drew on these weaker areas. Her natural pattern of growth at midlife would involve developing her less-preferred function, and indeed that's what happened.

God has planted in us the desire to grow, and at midlife we are driven to use our least-preferred functions as a part of our growth. A wise pastor, using type to help parishioners find direction for service at midlife, might make some very subtle suggestions nudging people in the direction of developing their least-preferred functions.

Let's imagine that Janine, the INTJ who loves administration in the theater, is in her 40s or 50s and has expressed to her pastor some discontent with doing the same kinds of things she's been doing all her adult life. She says her life feels small; something is missing. Her pastor could consider Janine's least-preferred functions—sensing and feeling. The pastor could suggest to Janine that she experiment with delegating a few of the administrative tasks for the next play, tasks which Janine would normally enjoy a great deal, and instead take on one or two new tasks that draw on sensing and feeling, such as bringing food to a rehearsal, praying with people in need, or trying to listen carefully and sympathetically when people express their feelings.

In *God's Gifted People*, Gary Harbaugh describes the SF "gift of personal helpfulness."[2] The SF strengths are related to the practical supports that people need in order to fit together. These are the strengths that Janine, an NT, has probably not developed very much. The pastor could brainstorm with Janine regarding other ways she could develop her SF side by considering avenues of service that meet practical people needs in ways that might feel at least somewhat natural to Janine.

Midlife is an excellent time to read descriptions of types that are opposite or nearly opposite to our own, drawing from those descriptions ideas of how to experiment with service in areas we've never before tried. A pastor or church leader can do the same for anyone whose type is known, thus providing growth challenges in new areas at the time when they are most needed.

Type and Serving

Many factors lead us to a place of service. Often our passions, our values, and our commitments lead us to a specific ministry, as in Elizabeth's case when she got involved with hospice. We can help congregation members identify these powerful forces as a guide to service.[3]

Sometimes we choose a place of service to balance our work environment, as John did. Sometimes we stumble into a ministry simply because it needs to be done or because one of our friends is involved.

Once we begin serving in a specific ministry, type can give us understanding and insight into why certain tasks are enjoyable and others are not. Type can help us make choices within that ministry to bring balance to our lives. Understanding type can help us know when to delegate tasks to someone else. Type can help us know when to ask for help.

A pastor or lay leader who understands type can help congregation members in their ministries. Understanding type enables us to give more effective support when congregation members are struggling in their ministries. We can ask questions and brainstorm solutions more effectively when we understand type.

Type alone usually does not guide us into a path of service, but it can provide wisdom in many ways after we get there.

CHAPTER 3

Stewarding Our Gifts

"I say to everyone among you not to think of yourself more highly than you ought to think, but to think with sober judgment, each according to the measure of faith that God has assigned. For as in one body we have many members, and not all the members have the same function, so we, who are many, are one body in Christ, and individually we are members one of another" (Romans 12:3-5).

The four New Testament passages that address spiritual gifts have important truths to teach us. These truths form an excellent foundation for teaching about type in congregations. The passage in Romans addresses our tendency to think more highly of ourselves than of other people. As we identify the special way God has made and gifted us, we are tempted to think that our gifts are the most important ones. Instead, as the Apostle Paul teaches, we are to embrace the truth that even though different people in the community have different functions, we are all part of one body and so connected to each other that we cannot negate the value of each other's contributions.

The brief passage on spiritual gifts in 1 Peter 4:10 presents our responsibility to use our gifts faithfully. "Like good stewards of the manifold grace of God, serve one another with whatever gift each of you has received." The goal, according to verse 11, is that "God may be glorified in all things through Christ Jesus." We are commanded to steward the gifts we have been given. The way we do that is to use them to serve others, and the end result is that God will be glorified.

Ephesians 4:11-13 addresses the purpose of the use of spiritual gifts within the body of Christ. God gave to the church apostles, prophets, evangelists, pastors, and teachers "to equip the saints for ministry, for building up the body of Christ, until all of us come to the unity of faith and of the knowledge of the Son of God, to maturity, to the measure of the full stature of Christ." These words state a clear mandate that church leaders are to serve the members of the body by helping them discover and use their own gifts effectively in ministry. The long-term goal is maturity and unity.

Chapters 12 and 14 of 1 Corinthians discuss many aspects of spiritual gifts. The two chapters are sandwiched around 1 Corinthians 13, the famous love chapter, which is beautiful and instructive standing alone. It is also very helpful to consider the implications of that chapter as a corrective in the midst of complicated discussions about individual giftedness. We need a constant reminder of the primacy of love in our lives as we attempt to use our gifts to minister to people.

Verses 4 to 7 of 1 Corinthians 12 affirm that there are varieties of gifts, services, and activities, but there is only one Lord and God. One Holy Spirit activates all these gifts. These varieties of ministries are given for the common good.

Verses 14 to 26 make an extended comparison between the gifts in the body of Christ and the parts of our physical body. We need both eyes and feet; our body wouldn't work if we had only eyes or only feet. We cover up some parts of the body, and other parts of the body are completely hidden inside, yet they are all indispensable.

These verses are particularly comforting to introverts, who sometimes feel that their ministry of prayer and quiet caring go unnoticed because these gifts seem to be invisible. Church leaders who enjoy upfront, highly verbal leadership styles need to read and meditate on these verses of 1 Corinthians 12 and then give affirmation and support to those who minister quietly and behind the scenes.

Correlating Spiritual Gifts and Type

The passages described above can be used effectively in congregations when either type or spiritual gifts (or both!) are taught. We all need reminders of our call to embrace diversity while we affirm the unity of faith. We need to be encouraged to be good stewards of everything God has given us, including our spiritual gifts. Those of us in church leadership need encouragement to use our gifts in the body for the purpose of enabling others to minister. These passages are a gold mine when teaching about type or gifts in a congregation.

Each of the four passages also mentions specific gifts, and that's where the complications start. A survey of books in religious bookstores will reveal that these lists of specific gifts are treated differently by different authors. If a leader wants to teach about both type and spiritual gifts, it is essential to understand these different views of the lists of gifts the New Testament passages contain.

All the Gifts Are Alike

Church growth expert C. Peter Wagner, in *Your Spiritual Gifts Can Help Your Church Grow,*[1] presents the viewpoint that all the lists of gifts describe spiritual gifts that are essentially alike. These gifts, according to Wagner, are alike in that they are all given at conversion, we "have" them throughout our Christian life, we are called to use them faithfully, and we can abuse them if we aren't careful. Non-Christians cannot have these gifts, he believes, and all the gifts listed in the New Testament are unrelated to our natural abilities and talents. Wagner defines a spiritual gift as "a special attribute given by the Holy Spirit to every member of the Body of Christ according to God's grace for use within the context of the body."

Wagner believes that the lists of gifts in the four passages cover most of the gifts that God has given to the church. He adds a few: voluntary poverty, martyrdom, intercession, missionary, and exorcism. He adds this handful of gifts based on what he has observed about the way the church around the world works. The popular Houts questionnaire, a spiritual gifts inventory which can be purchased at some Christian bookstores, is based on most of the same presuppositions as C. Peter Wagner presented.

The Gifts Lists Are Different

Other authors believe that each of the biblical texts describes a different kind of gift. The passage in Ephesians 4:11 is clearly about gifts given to serve within the Christian body; in this view, Ephesians 4 presents a list of roles in the church.

The gifts described in 1 Corinthians 12 and 14 are gifts given in worship at the direction of the Holy Spirit. People don't "have" these gifts in a lasting sense; these gifts are given as needed for a specific worship situation.

The gifts described in Romans 12:6-8 are yet another kind of gift. These are gifts that we have our whole life long; these gifts are amplified and brought under the Holy Spirit's control when we become Christians, but we can see them in children. Don and Katie Fortune, writing out of their background in Pentecostal churches, call the Romans 12 gifts "motivational gifts," and they present this view clearly and persuasively in *Discover Your God-Given Gifts.*[2] Their book contains detailed questionnaires covering only the Romans 12 gifts, and they have many helpful ideas on the appropriate use of these gifts.

The Gifts Lists Are "For Example"

To understand this third view, consider these three statements: Mount Fuji and Mount Everest are mountains. Mountain climbing on Mont Blanc and Les Dents du Midi is good exercise. Mountains, particularly Mount Rainier and Mount McKinley, brighten up the landscape in the western United States.

Each of the three statements lists two or more mountains, but there are many more than six mountains in the world. Each list is slightly different because each focuses on a different geographic area, but none of the lists claims to be exhaustive, either of the mountains in that part of the world or of all mountains in all the world.

In the same way, this third view of spiritual gifts presents the idea that the lists of gifts in the Bible simply cite examples of gifts used in different areas of life. Harbaugh, in *God's Gifted People*, seems to adopt this view. He summarizes the four New Testament gifts passages with three conclusions: that God is the giver of all gifts, that gifts are given to be used to serve others, and that "each individual person is in some way gifted by God."[3] He presents psychological type as a way we are gifted by God.

Teaching Type and Spiritual Gifts

One way to use the passages about spiritual gifts is to adopt Gary Harbaugh's point of view and take the general principles from the passages and then teach type as a way of describing how we are gifted. This method, however, ignores the lists of specific gifts.

Another way to teach type and spiritual gifts is to view the spiritual gifts lists as one angle on human giftedness, with psychological type as another way of looking at the complex sculpture that is human personality. Jane Kise, David Stark, and Sandra Hirsh, in *LifeKeys*, present type and spiritual gifts as two of five areas to consider when seeking to find a place to serve in congregations.

A third way to teach type and gifts is to try to correlate the specific spiritual gifts with type. A number of Doctor of Ministry dissertations have been written on this topic. Some of them present extremely complex schemes.

In the courses I've taught covering both type and spiritual gifts, I have noticed a few patterns. Most people with the gift of compassion have a preference for feeling. Many people with the gift of administration have preferences for TJ. But that's about all I've observed. I am unwilling to try very hard to correlate type and gifts. I have found helpful insights about Christian service from books written from both Wagner's and the Fortunes' viewpoints. I don't want to adopt the third viewpoint and completely ignore the specific lists of gifts found in the New Testament. But neither do I want to try to correlate the lists of spiritual gifts with the categories of type. I am much more comfortable with the idea that type and spiritual gifts look at human personality from different angles.

Key truths about the diversity of human giftedness are found in the spiritual gifts passages: one God, many ways of doing things, the call to steward our gifts, the call to appreciate people who are different than we are. These truths provide a foundation for teaching on spiritual gifts, and they also provide an undergirding for an understanding of the diversity of personality as described by type.

We are called to use our gifts and talents carefully, as stewards of what God has given us. Sometimes we use these gifts and talents all too well, to the point of overuse. As we discuss stewarding our gifts, we also have to consider the issue of burnout, because burnout so powerfully destroys our ability to serve using our gifts.

Burnout

Bonnie and Rick are co-pastors of a small congregation. They are also husband and wife and parents of two boys in elementary school. Bonnie has type preferences for ENTJ. Her style of living is fast-paced and organized. She is a strategist and organizer above all. She manages the checkbook at home and the stewardship campaign at church. She oversees the family social calendar and keeps track of coming events at church. She even enjoys attending meetings, particularly when she can lead them.

Rick, who has INFP preferences, excels as a listener. He comes across as careful and attentive, the kind of person who will take all the time necessary to listen and express caring. His boys know they can talk to him about anything. His parishioners bring their hurts and pain to him. He has an extraordinary ability to come alongside people, to be present with them in pain, listening without judgment or the need to fix anything in their lives.

Bonnie and Rick have been careful stewards of their own gifts, using them to serve and care for others. In addition, Bonnie and Rick respect each other's gifts. They have built a pattern of marriage and career that has worked well for many years. They rely on each other's strengths. They affirm each other's gifts. They are faithful to the spirit of 1 Corinthians 12; they value the diversity of each other's gifts, and they affirm that these gifts come from God. They are grateful to have a partnership in which each person can compensate for the other's weaknesses. Bonnie is grateful that Rick handles the pastoral care needs at church, because pastoral counseling drains her. Rick is grateful that Bonnie handles scheduling and finances at home and at work, because he finds such details boring.

It seems like a perfect partnership, yet after 12 years of marriage and eight years of shared ministry, Bonnie and Rick are increasingly irritable with each other and increasingly overloaded by their home and work lives. Each day they are moving closer to burnout. What could possibly be wrong?

Burnout from Overuse

There are many causes of burnout. Probably the most easily observed comes when we are using less preferred areas too much, particularly without lots of support and encouragement. We get tired. An accumulation of fatigue burns us out.

Bonnie and Rick's situation illustrates another source of burnout which is harder to understand at first. After all, they have divided up their work life so that both of them are using their gifts. They excel at what they do. They respect each other's strengths. Why would they be starting to burn out?

According to some trainers who work with clergy, more of them burn out because of overusing of their strengths than any other factor. The common pattern goes like this: A new clergyperson arrives at a congregation. At first he does a wide variety of tasks, trying to find his place in the congregation. He excels at certain tasks and he gets a lot of praise for doing those tasks, so he does them more and more. The tasks he excels at are the ones that come from his gifts and his strengths.

Some lay leaders follow this same pattern, experiencing burnout because of overusing their strengths. This is particularly true for lay leaders when their jobs draw heavily on the same strengths they use in their volunteering.

Burnout can be like carpal tunnel syndrome or repetitive motion syndrome. Overuse of one part of our body results in soreness and pain. By the time we experience the pain, the pattern of motion has been in place for a very long time. It's hard to change the pattern, and it's hard to receive healing because the pattern of motion is so deeply ingrained in the way we move our bodies.

Overuse of our gifts and strengths in ministry follows the same pattern as repetitive motion syndrome. By the time we experience pain, the pattern of overuse is firmly established. Whether we are a pastor or a lay leader, the congregation expects us to continue to perform in the areas where we have shown so much competence. It is extremely difficult to form new patterns of behavior.

To understand the way type can help us avoid this type of burnout, it is helpful to look again at the human body. My son played baseball every year from Little League up through high school. He played catcher for many years, enjoying that position very much because of the intimate involvement in the strategy of the game.

Unfortunately, his arm couldn't keep up with the demands of throwing to second base. By the time his team had advanced to the larger baseball diamond, his arm gave him so much trouble that he routinely took painkillers before games. In high school he played catcher only occasionally because of the chronic pain in his arm.

My husband found some articles describing exercises my son could do during the off-season to strengthen his arm. The exercises did not involve his arm directly. The goal was to strengthen his shoulder muscles, so that the arm would be more effectively supported by the surrounding muscles.

The same principle applies to avoiding burnout by considering type. Let's look back at Bonnie and Rick. Bonnie is overusing her dominant function of extraverted thinking. She uses thinking to organize the calendar, finances, and just about everything else, both at home and at work. She probably uses her auxiliary function, intuition, quite a bit because much of the extraverted thinking she does involves planning ahead and looking at the future and draws on her intuition. But her less-preferred functions which we could call supporting functions—sensing and feeling—are underused. Her thinking "muscle" is not well supported by the surrounding muscles.

The same applies to Rick. He uses his dominant, introverted feeling all the time in his caring and listening. His auxiliary function, extraverted intuition, also comes into play because he seeks to remain open to whatever people want to share with him. He is open to possibilities and future goals in people's lives. But the two other functions, sensing and thinking, find little place in Rick's life. He, like Bonnie, is not developing the supporting muscles.

What could they do?

A place to start in addressing burnout—but not a final solution—is to consider recreational activities. Bonnie could ask herself how she could use sensing and feeling during her time off. Rick could ask the same question about sensing and thinking.

Since sensing is a function both of them need to develop, they could ask themselves how they could use sensing more in their life of play. Maybe they could hike in the country on their days off, trying to be very attentive to sensory stimuli. Maybe they could refinish some furniture together. Maybe they could take a family art class with their sons. Maybe they could cook together, using exotic and extremely precise recipes.

Maybe they could work together in their garden, seeking to enjoy the smells and colors of the plants and the texture and feel of the dirt.

Cooking, art, and gardening can draw on any of the functions. Bonnie and Rick would need to focus consciously on staying in the present in these activities—noticing the smells, tastes, colors, and sounds—as they seek to develop their sensing function in the midst of these activities.

Each of them could read a description of their exact opposite. For Bonnie it would be ISFP and for Rick it would be ESTJ. They could look for patterns of recreation that are common for those types and then experiment with new recreational activities.

In the long run, meeting these needs only through recreation will probably not be enough. It will also be necessary to find places at work to draw on these less-preferred functions. Since both of them have preferences for intuition, there are probably many sensing tasks both at home and at church that neither of them has been involved with. Maybe one or both of them could get involved in helping to decorate the church or in cooking or cleaning up for a church meal.

In addition, they both need to find small ways to develop their inferior function—thinking for Rick and feeling for Bonnie. They will need to permit the other person to take on some new tasks. Bonnie may need to let Rick take on some planning tasks that he simply won't do as well as she does. Likewise, Bonnie may need to do some more pastoral care and listening. They definitely shouldn't take on many hours of these tasks, and they shouldn't add these tasks to their existing job descriptions, but each of them could replace a few things they do very well with a few tasks they find more difficult.

Both Bonnie and Rick could experiment with prayer forms based on their least-preferred functions. They could seek to incorporate the skills of these least-preferred functions when they study the Bible.

Taking on tasks that come easily to us feels natural and right. We get positive feedback, and we know that we are making a positive contribution. On the surface and at the beginning, it seems that we are being wise stewards of the gifts God has given us. Yet in order to avoid burnout and in order to be long-term stewards of our gifts, we need to be careful that we are engaging in some tasks that draw on our less-preferred functions.

This raises theological issues. When we work only in our areas of strength, we might begin to become convinced that we are like God in our competence and strength. When we make room for tasks that don't come easily for us, we will need to rely on God more and we will be reminded that we are finite creatures. Pastors need to help other pastors avoid burnout through overuse of their strengths. Lay people need to encourage pastors to grow in weaker areas.

Because some lay people also experience burnout from overuse of their strengths, pastors need to help them evaluate the use of their strengths. As we help parishioners involved in service, we need to watch carefully for patterns of overuse of strengths, particularly if the person serving in the congregation is duplicating many of the skills used at work. It's important to encourage people to take on tasks that will stretch them. It's important to give them the freedom to blunder around a little bit. In the short run, church programs might not run as smoothly, but in the long run volunteers won't burn out as fast.

Burnout from Frustration and Stress

Carrie's story illustrates a very different cause of burnout. Carrie, an energetic corporate executive with ESTJ preferences, got involved in the youth ministry at her church because she had become a Christian in a high school youth group she attended with a friend. She feels strongly about ministering to youth.

Carrie heard that there were plenty of volunteers to run the youth group, but that there were vacancies on the youth ministry committee. She believed her gifts would be used effectively in a committee setting, so she agreed to join the committee. Her organizational skills became evident immediately. She was asked to take on the task of developing a policy manual.

The youth director had ENFP preferences, and most of the committee members also had NF preferences. The youth group was a warm and friendly place, and lives were being changed because of the accepting atmosphere, but the lack of clear policies was becoming a problem. The church van was frequently requested for outings by families within the church. The youth classrooms were used by youth group members for all kinds of activities that had nothing to do with the church. Some kids had been caught smoking marijuana behind the church building during a youth group meeting, and no disciplinary action had been taken.

Carrie dived into the task of developing the policy manual. She called six other churches to talk with youth directors about their policies. She presented several drafts of the manual to the youth committee, asking for input so she could make revisions. The committee discussed the manual briefly each time she presented a draft to them and praised her verbally for the good job she was doing. Finally, after about six months, the manual was complete. Carrie was proud of her work. The manual was concise and concrete, covering policies in several areas.

As the months went by, Carrie's pride turned to frustration. The manual was almost never used. Decisions continued to be made on a case-by-case basis. Several times during committee meetings, when decisions needed to be made that were covered by the manual, Carrie cited the policy they had already established. She was ignored. Deeply hurt, she left the committee and ultimately left the church.

Oddly enough, as the months and years went by, the policies in the manual became a part of the youth group's structure. Carrie didn't stay around long enough to see her work implemented.

It's easy to see in retrospect that the committee shouldn't have asked Carrie to create something that they had no real intention of implementing. But the youth pastor and the committee members didn't understand how deeply rooted was their NF pattern of trying to enable each person—on an individual basis—to achieve what that person wanted and needed. They thought they wanted policies, but the policies seemed narrow, rigid, and confining in the first months after they were presented.

It would have been helpful at any point in the process of developing the policy manual for a few more people with ST, SF, and NT preferences to be recruited to the youth committee. It would have been helpful if someone had been able to observe and describe the NF pattern of decisionmaking so everyone could understand the obstacles that would have to be overcome to implement a policy manual. Carrie received words of gratitude, which the committee viewed as affirmation of her work, but the affirmation she craved was the implementation of her work. Neither she nor the committee understood the patterns at play.

The kind of powerlessness that Carrie felt can be experienced by laypeople when pastors or groups are too controlling, and lay leaders are unable to exercise true leadership. No one would call this particular youth pastor controlling; he is warm and affectionate and shares leadership willingly with the youth leaders. Yet the predominant NF type of most of the youth committee members had the effect of controlling the way the group operated. Bringing that pattern out into the light of day and discussing it openly would have been immensely helpful for Carrie, as well as for the pastor and committee members.

There are many sources of frustration that can cause burnout for lay leaders. Another common experience is lack of clear expectations when someone is recruited to serve on a leadership board.

Sam, with ISTJ preferences, was elected to serve on the vestry in his Episcopal congregation. He was fairly new to the congregation, but he was one of only a few people in their 30s. He knew he was elected to represent his age group and to help the church attract more people his age.

At first he felt lost at the vestry meetings. Everyone was discussing issues that he knew nothing about. He assumed it would get better, and as the months went by he began to enter into the discussions. But he still had no idea what he was supposed to do. Once he was asked to serve on a task force to figure out a better way to organize the coffee hours. It was an easy task, accomplished in a short period of time.

After six months on the vestry, he went to the rector, a warm and outgoing man named Hal who had ENTP preferences. Sam told Hal he was frustrated being on the vestry because he had no idea what he was supposed to be doing. Hal told Sam he was doing fine. Sam said he didn't feel like he was doing fine; in fact, he didn't feel like he was doing anything.

Hal talked with Sam about leadership and vision. Hal said he valued the input from the vestry very highly. He told Sam that just by being there, just by contributing to the discussions, he was contributing to the direction of the church.

Sam didn't feel any better after that discussion. He still didn't feel that he was doing anything. A few months later he raised the same issue with Hal who again assured him that he was participating in setting the vision for the congregation. Sam finished his term on the vestry because he wanted to be faithful, but the three years of frustration dulled him and left him drained of energy.

Somewhere between one-half and three-quarters of the people in North American congregations have preferences for sensing. Close to two-thirds of the clergy in American congregations have preferences for intuition. This is a recipe for frustration for lay leaders.

Many intuitives are uncomfortable with job descriptions. Written task descriptions feel limiting. Having everything laid out feels like it restricts creativity. Describing a congregational leadership role in concrete terms feels too narrow. Many intuitives like to figure things out on their own. Having a detailed job description can take the fun out of doing the task. Therefore, many clergy, particularly those with preferences for intuition, don't want to give lay leaders too much concrete instruction about their roles because they don't want to stifle them.

Many sensors, and some intuitives, are not comfortable stepping into an amorphous situation. Many sensors crave concrete instruction. The words "leadership" and "vision" have very little meaning without specific task descriptions. The common pattern of congregational leadership boards, operating without job descriptions or task lists, can make sensors feel extremely uneasy. In the end they cannot measure their accomplishments because there were no goals set out for them.

The job description of a leadership board member could be as simple as a handful of concrete responsibilities: to pray regularly for the congregation's ministries and its leaders, to listen carefully to parishioner concerns and bring them to the board, to attend all board meetings unless there are extenuating circumstances, and to take on specific tasks when asked. Having these responsibilities laid out clearly will relieve anxiety in the short run and will help avoid frustration and burnout in the long run.

Being a Volunteer-Friendly Congregation

In many congregations, clergy and leaders spend a lot of time trying to help their parishioners find comfortable places to serve. We need to spend an equal amount of time and energy trying to become a congregation that is a rewarding place to serve. This will enable the community to be a good steward of the spiritual gifts and talents among its members, and it will be a place that encourages members to be good stewards of their own gifts.

We've already seen two possible pitfalls that type can help address. In Carrie's case, if someone had been able to describe the type forces at work, the whole committee might have understood what was happening when they had such a hard time implementing the policy manual. Understanding type might have helped Carrie get the affirmation she needed.

In Sam's case, if some specific items had been written in a job description, he would have been more likely to thrive as a vestry member.

Let's consider each of the type preferences in order to outline some of the ways in which a congregation can become volunteer-friendly.

Extraversion

Many extraverts will be most comfortable volunteering with a group of people. A monthly or quarterly Saturday morning group that gathers to do building repairs will probably be more attractive to an extravert than volunteering to do a repair task alone. Does the congregation promote group volunteer opportunities such as mission trips?

Some congregations are so geared to introverts that the only tasks advertised are those that must be done independently, alone or in small groups. Extraverts will more likely want to join a group of people working on a project.

Many extraverts love to pray for their congregation. A prayer chain can appeal to extraverts because it enables them to feel connected to the people's needs. Prayer meetings and prayer in small group meetings can appeal to extraverts.

Introversion

Introverts often like to serve in quiet settings with a small number of people. If the congregation only offers large-scale volunteer projects, such as building houses for Habitat for Humanity or serving in a children's program with lots of children and adults involved, then introverts may not want to volunteer.

Does the congregation advertise quiet, behind-the-scenes tasks that need to be done? Are there helpful projects that could be accomplished by an individual or a very small group of people working independently? Does the congregation affirm that such tasks are important? Do behind-the-scenes volunteers get recognition and affirmation?

Just as important, does the congregation value prayer as a significant ministry? Is there public acknowledgment that people who pray for the ministries are upholding the congregation in a deeply important way? Some people will want to pray at home for prayer requests. Is there a prayer chain or some other way to inform them of prayer needs?

Sensing

As we noted above, sensors often appreciate concrete instructions for tasks. Are there written job descriptions for leadership positions? Do the committees have job descriptions or statements of purpose?

Are concrete tasks valued? Congregational activities wouldn't happen without someone to set up chairs, wash dishes, create decorations, and proofread written material. Are these tasks valued? Are people who serve in concrete, "small" ways encouraged and thanked? Is there public acknowledgment that without people to serve in these areas, the ministry would be seriously compromised?

Because the majority of clergy prefer intuition, and because intuitives often don't notice these practical tasks, in many congregations there is the real possibility that sensors aren't thanked and appreciated enough

Intuition

In many congregations the pastor holds the keys to vision and doesn't allow anyone else to participate in setting direction or discussing larger issues. This situation can be death for intuitives.

Most intuitives enjoy settings where they can participate in the creation of vision, but this need is particularly acute for extraverted intuitives who do their best visioning in a group brainstorming discussion. Introverted intuitives, on the other hand, often come up with their visions during prayer or other time alone, but they need settings where they can describe what they have thought about and receive affirmation. Do committee meetings focus only on details, or is there an opportunity to discuss long-range vision from time to time? Is the board encouraged to dream together about the congregation's direction? Are there open forums from time to time to discuss vision in specific areas of ministry?

Thinking

When people have a preference for thinking, they often want their ideas and plans to be evaluated apart from themselves. Carrie, who created the policy manual, was completely willing to do the work if it was appreciated and implemented. The other people on the committee, those who had preferences for feeling, gave her words of affirmation and acceptance. Carrie didn't want or need personal affirmation; she wanted her work itself to be recognized. The best affirmation that Carrie could receive would be the implementation of the policies in the manual. If that weren't possible, then engagement and discussion about the manual would have felt affirming to Carrie. Analytical thinking about her proposal would probably have been taken as a compliment.

The judging function—thinking and feeling—is the arena where the most hurt feelings arise. Thinking types usually have a detachment from the people involved in the situation; they often want to focus on the plan or program apart from people's feelings. But those who prefer thinking can be hurt. We know that God cares for people, so it seems natural to affirm feeling. We also need to affirm that God cares equally for truth. If we don't, then the people who prefer thinking will feel second-class.

Most churches do a fairly good job of publicizing the service opportunities that draw on sensing and thinking, such as building repair, accounting, and financial positions. It's more difficult to find places where intuition and thinking can be used. People with NT preferences excel at analysis. Is there a place for analysis and program planning on the part of laypeople, or does the staff hold all the power to make plans and analyze existing programs? Is there a setting where NT gifts can be used to do long-term planning or analyze existing programs?

Feeling

People with feeling preferences will often be able to find a comfortable place to serve, whether it's holding a baby in the nursery or serving the seniors at a brunch or learning listening skills in a Stephen Ministry setting. There are so many people who need serving in congregations and so many places where people needs are paramount.

People who prefer feeling often need to be thanked and appreciated. Sometimes in congregational ministries the people with thinking preferences end up being in charge because they have the administrative interests and gifts to run programs. They may not have the need to be personally thanked and appreciated, so they forget to communicate their gratitude to the people who work in their ministry area. For someone who prefers feeling, one-to-one thanks, either in person or in a handwritten note, can be more important than being listed in a newsletter article or being given a certificate at a public gathering.

For people who prefer feeling, the most important consideration is usually the needs of the people around them. This can contrast greatly with people who prefer thinking and are concerned with competence, excellence, and truth, even if the needs of people must be compromised to get there. The different needs and concerns of thinkers and feelers need to be taken into account when ministries are established and evaluated.

Judging

People with a preference for judging need a certain amount of predictability and structure. Clear job descriptions will usually appeal to people with a judging preference. Clear time lines and expectations usually help them serve without anxiety. If a pastor or ministry leader has preferences for perceiving, he or she needs to be extra careful to provide the kind of structure that people with judging preferences need. He or she also needs to work hard to follow through on commitments.

Perceiving

Patterns of dealing with new information are a key consideration when seeking ministries that will probably be comfortable for a person with perceiving preferences. Is there a way to continue to receive information after a decision has been made? Is there a willingness to incorporate that information? When plans are made, are they set in concrete or is there a certain amount of flexibility to respond to new needs and issues as they come up?

A pastor or lay leader with judging preferences needs to be careful that plans don't suffocate people with perceiving preferences.

We can present workshops on finding a place to serve by using type and spiritual gifts, but laypeople can still be frustrated if the congregation provides service opportunities only for certain types. Many congregations have tangible tasks that appeal to STs and SFs. Are there also places that NTs and NFs can help create vision?

Does the leadership board, where intuition is usually most valued in congregations, provide concrete job descriptions so that the sensing types can feel comfortable in that setting?

Are there quiet tasks that can be done alone, in pairs, or in small groups? Are there opportunities for group service?

Are there plenty of ways volunteers are thanked? Is there appreciation of the actual work people have done?

Is there structure and predictability in ministry tasks? Is there a way to remain flexible after plans are made?

All of these will help to make a congregation volunteer-friendly and allow people with diverse gifts and personality types to find a place to serve. All of these will enable members to be good stewards of their gifts.

CHAPTER 4

Prayer and Bible Study

Caroline, an energetic, 20-something ENTJ who works in a busy stock-broker's office, always signs up for the quiet day retreats at her church. These retreats, which are held two or three times per year, provide lots of individual time to pray, as well as time for Scripture readings, guided meditations, and corporate worship.

When Caroline first understood the principles of type, she reflected, "I don't understand how I can be so comfortable at the quiet day retreats if I'm an extravert. I thought extraverts prefer action and lots of activity. I do like to be busy, but I also value my quiet moments. These quiet day retreats provide a wonderful structure for me. There's enough variety to keep me going but there's lots of time alone. Why do I enjoy this so much if I'm an extravert?"

Norma, on the other hand, a homemaker in her early 40s with ENFP preferences, has absolutely no interest in attending the quiet day retreats. "When there's silence in worship or at a retreat, I get nervous. I have quiet times at home when I read the Bible and pray, and that's enough silent spirituality for me. I meet God best with other people. That's why I'm in a small home-group and that's why I volunteer at the tutoring program we have."

How can we respond to these two extraverts who have such different experiences of silent prayer? First, their stories illustrate the danger of making generalizations about type. We can describe common patterns of expressing type, but people are all incredibly different. We need to say things like "extraverts often . . ." and "extraverts may find themselves . . ." rather than making dogmatic pronouncements.

In the realm of individual prayer, this is particularly true. God can meet us through our strengths or our weaknesses, and type helps offer a vocabulary to describe the range of options.

Understanding Type and Prayer

In 1983 and 1984 two ground-breaking books were published: *From Image to Likeness*[1] and *Prayer and Temperament*.[2] Isabel Briggs Myers' 1980 book, *Gifts Differing*,[3] had described the basics of personality type, with applications in learning style, marriage, and careers. These two new books introduced some connections between personality type and spiritual development. They were a wonderful challenge to integrate faith with personality type.

From Image to Likeness presents four patterns of spirituality based on the four functions—intuition, sensing, thinking, and feeling. It also presents a pattern of type development over life. The authors suggest that we will develop each of the four functions at different times in our lives. The implication is that we will grow spiritually in different ways at different times.

The authors of *Prayer and Temperament* present four types of traditional Catholic prayer patterns and link them with the four temperament types. They write that the Ignatian pattern will suit SJs best. This is a discipline of trying to project oneself back into a biblical setting or event in history and trying to find personal meaning in it. NFs will find joy using the Augustinian method of transposing the words of Scripture into our world today using creative imagination. Franciscan spirituality, which will appeal to SPs, is optimistic and sees the presence of God in all of life. The authors describe Thomistic prayer as a logical and rational meditation which may involve concern with transcendent values such as truth, goodness, and beauty. They believe that the NT will have a special connection with this kind of prayer, which often appears not to be prayer at all, but looks more like study.

Bruce Duncan, writing about eight years later in *Pray Your Way*, presented a new idea that continued the dialogue and changed the paradigm presented in *Prayer and Temperament*. Duncan believes that we will all have a pattern of prayer that will be most comfortable for us, an everyday style of prayer that will most likely be based on our dominant function. But we will probably encounter God most intensely through our inferior or our tertiary function.

Duncan's idea was immensely helpful to me because it so accurately described my pattern of prayer. I pray all the time in an introverted intuitive way, based on my dominant function. I call it "thinking with God." It's a mess of ideas, thoughts, concerns about people, and plans for classes and sermons, interspersed with direct prayers for people and situations. If I don't take the time to pray that way during the day, I'll be awake in the night to do it. I can't live without it.

But the times when I meet God most intensely are related to extraverted sensing, my inferior function. I can experience overwhelming awe and wonder seeing a beam of sunlight coming through the window. The sunset behind the mountains, the feel of the water on my skin when I dive into a pool on a hot day, or the smell of a rose can give me a vivid sense of God's reality.

Duncan's paradigm completely changes the way we think about prayer in church communities. It is tempting to say that we need to have periods of quiet meditation on faith symbols for the introverted intuitives, and liturgical dance or beautiful banners for the extraverted sensors. The opposite is true if we meet God most directly through our inferior or tertiary function. The extraverted sensors may know that God is present in what they perceive through their senses. They experience that all the time. What they may need help with is meeting God through symbol and metaphor, in the prayer pattern of intuition. And it may be the introverted intuitives who will benefit most from looking at the beautiful banners.

We need to make sure that our congregations offer a wide variety of prayer experiences so that all types have the potential to meet God through any of their functions. We need to stop saying things like, "We have quiet periods in our worship so the introverts feel comfortable, and we have a coffee hour for the extraverts." We have quiet periods and coffee hours for both the introverts and extraverts, so they can find God in comfortable places, and so they can be surprised at the way God finds them in situations that are normally not as comfortable.

Eight Patterns of Prayer

In order to offer this variety of prayer experiences, we need to understand what prayer looks like when experienced in each of the four functions (sensing, intuition, thinking, and feeling) in each of the two attitudes (extraversion and introversion). Some of these prayer patterns may not fit our normally accepted views of prayer, but we need to expand our concept of prayer in order to allow people to meet God in a variety of ways.

Extraverted Sensing Prayer

"The heavens are telling the glory of God. . . . Day to day pours forth speech" (Psalm 19:1, 2).

Extraverted sensing prayer is rooted in sensory experiences of the world around us. God is present in the creation—real, tangible, and concrete. The wind whispers on our skin telling us God is everywhere. The heat of the sun surrounds us and warms us with God's ever-present love. The vivid colors of the fall leaves delight us and remind us of God's extravagance in making the world so beautiful. The sunset behind misty purple mountains sends us into awe and joy. The exquisite pleasure of the first bite of a perfectly prepared souffle, the complex pattern of melodies in a Bach organ fugue, a Siamese cat's graceful leap to the top of an eight-foot fence—all of these communicate the present reality of God and the presence of God's abundant love.

Extraverted sensing prayer involves the body. God can feel present when we use our muscles just the way they were intended when bending over to pull up a dandelion in the garden or when setting out on a long walk. God is present in the joy of skiing a perfect run or hitting a tennis ball right into the corner. The thrill of physical competence is experienced as a gift from God.

Why do we waste so much time talking and listening in worship? This is a question we ask when we are absorbed with extraverted sensing. Why don't we sing more, raising our hands and swaying our bodies? Why don't we have more liturgical dance? Why don't we decorate the sanctuary with an abundance of fresh flowers, vivid banners, and lots of candles? Why don't we use incense more often?

Extraverted sensing also connects us to service. We experience God right beside us in the midst of handing a plate of spaghetti to a homeless woman at a church dinner, as we look into the clear eyes of a child in the Sunday school class we're teaching, or as we hammer a nail into the wall of a Habitat for Humanity house. Being able to serve in concrete ways connects us to God, who upholds and sustains the physical creation every moment. When we are using extraverted sensing, this kind of service feels like prayer, because it is an offering to God.

Many people must stretch their concept of prayer to include the joy of skiing down a mountain or the experience of vivid physical sensations as gifts from God and as evidence of the presence of God. Yet we make prayer inaccessible to many when we limit times of prayer to sitting in a chair, praying in a group with our eyes closed, or using only words.

Many of the psalms include praise to God for the physical creation. As we enter the 21st century, in our era of interest in spirituality in all forms, we need to affirm the simple joys of seeing the Creator's hand in the beauty of creation.

Introverted Sensing Prayer

"On your wondrous works I will meditate" (Psalm 145:5).

Introverted sensing prayer is a quiet, reflective response to God, rooted in our inner sensations and memories. Introverted sensing uses the five senses in the mind. When we remember with thankfulness the specifics of a time that God worked in our lives, we are using introverted sensing. The cool, damp weather that day, the specific flavors in the meal of salmon, new potatoes, and nutty brownies we ate, the feel of the hug we received when the crisis was over and it was clear that God had worked everything out—all these memories rise up out of introverted sensing and enable us to remember and pray.

Using introverted sensing, we can return to a favorite cathedral or to the top of a mountain, places where we experienced the reality of God and connected with God personally and intimately. Using introverted sensing this way can be an excellent springboard to other kinds of prayer.

When we are using introverted sensing, we are grateful for our heritage and the traditions that inform our faith. Reginald Johnson, in *Your Personality and God*, describes the deeply meaningful projects undertaken by several introverted sensors that connected them to their heritage. One woman made a spiritual family tree, tracing back for several generations the people who had influenced her faith. Another person made a scale model of his childhood church. Others made spiritual pilgrimages to places where God had met them in the past.[4]

Structured prayer appeals to us when we are using introverted sensing. We may be drawn to using the Lord's Prayer, a psalm, a litany, or a piece of worship liturgy, memorizing and meditating on each line.

Introverted sensing enables us to place ourselves in the setting of Gospel stories and to meet Jesus face to face, as suggested by Saint Ignatius. We can imagine the smell of dust in the air, the press of the crowd against us, the weariness on the faces of the people waiting to be healed. Then it's our turn, and we approach Jesus and encounter him. We see the warm smile on his face, we feel the gentle touch of his hand, and we know that we are deeply loved. In turn, we smile at him and thank him for all his gifts to us.

Some forms of introverted sensing prayer seem acceptable and "normal," such as slowly praying the Lord's Prayer or imagining ourselves in a biblical story. Many would have trouble believing that making a scale model of a childhood church could be prayer, yet making that model can be an intense experience of remembering the goodness of God with thankfulness. Throughout much of the Old Testament, God's people are commanded to remember God's works. Their sin and disobedience arose when they forgot all that God had done. Remembering the hand of God in our lives can be an important part of drawing near to God in prayer.

Extraverted Intuitive Prayer

"Great is the Lord, and greatly to be praised; his greatness is unsearchable. . . . The might of your awesome deeds shall be proclaimed, and I will declare your greatness" (Psalm 145:3, 6).

Extraverted intuitive prayer involves the application of vision, inspiration, and ingenuity for the purpose of furthering God's kingdom in the world. When we are using extraverted intuition, we look at problems and obstacles, and we are able to create a way through, around, or over the hindrance. This solution comes from a flash of insight, and it is often a big-picture vision of what could be, addressing immediate problems but also embracing wider goals and broader dreams.

In prayer we use extraverted intuition when we pray about God's kingdom breaking into our hurting world with power, majesty, and love. Extraverted intuitive prayer is the prayer of great visions and grand inspirations for the purpose of making known God's greatness and love. Extraverted intuition isn't content with Band-Aids or a compromising style of problem solving; extraverted intuition wants to move forward toward the very best of the way things could be.

When we are using extraverted intuition, we are open to "a flow of impressions, hunches, inspirations, flashes of insight, bursts of creativity, imaginative leaps, and breakthrough discoveries,"[5] which can lead to ingenious solutions to challenges or to grand visions for moving the church forward. Challenges are the fuel that keeps extraverted intuition moving forward, and it lends itself to brainstorming with a group, then praying about all the possibilities.

When we are using extraverted intuition, we value freedom and autonomy. In the Christian context, it is extraverted intuition that enables us to see past structures and institutions, right into the heart of the Gospel that was given for the whole world.

Extraverted intuition is probably the most optimistic of the functions. When we pray with hope and expectancy—knowing that God will break through into the situation, seeing possibilities and visions for people and for programs, and being sure God will work the best in those situations—we are probably using extraverted intuition. When we long to be used by God to change the world—when we pray to be the agents of God's love on a large scale in the world—we are probably using extraverted intuition.

One part of healing prayer is extraverted intuitive prayer. When we pray for healing for someone—whether it's inner healing of memories or outer healing of the body—we need to see the person whole and well, and we need to pray in the light of that future. It is extraverted intuition that enables us to see that future hope of wholeness and well-being.

Because of the visions generated by extraverted intuition, it is tempting to see it as a "doing" function, but in reality it is a perceiving function. It is our ability to perceive possibilities and dreams on a grand scale and for the benefit of the world. Without these dreams we lose inspiration and hope, so it is important for all of us to experiment with prayer in the style of extraverted intuition.

Introverted Intuitive Prayer

"You are clothed with honor and majesty, wrapped in light as with a garment" (Psalm 104:1, 2).

Introverted intuitive prayer is like walking along a beach, looking at all the driftwood and shells brought in by the waves. It is like an overgrown, tangled garden, with fragrant flowers growing here and there on the ends of long, twining stems. Bruce Duncan calls intuitive prayer "butterfly prayer."[6] That term is particularly appropriate for introverted intuitive prayer in which our minds flit from one thought to the next, looking for patterns or keys that provide insight, inspiration, and vision. It's a process of thinking or meditating in God's presence, and the fruits of introverted intuitive prayer include insights about people, plans, direction, congregational life, family life, and so on.

Introverted intuitive prayer often draws on the symbols and metaphors of faith. A variety of names for God will provide fuel for this kind of prayer: God as rock, fortress, water of life, loving father, nurturing mother, or bread of life. Complex images such as the vineyard in John 15 can provide images from which to launch into butterfly prayer. This rich image of Jesus as the vine and the Father as the vine dresser might give us insight into God's work in our lives and we might feel our hearts open to God for a brief moment of true adoration and worship.

Or we might begin with this picture of the vineyard and move into considering the water source for vine and branches. Where did the water come from in the Middle East? Streams? Underground springs? Rain? Then, out of the blue, we might have a flash of insight about why our small group is stuck in a conflict regarding the role of Bible study in the group. The image of drawing up water makes the issue clear to us: some members of the group find nourishment in studying Scripture in great detail, and others find nourishment in personal sharing. This pattern of free association resulting in insight is typical for introverted intuitive prayer.

When we are able to pray about the present in the light of the future, we are probably using introverted intuitive prayer. This kind of prayer enables us to see to the essence of things and people in the light of what they will become. Introverted intuition can provide fuel for powerful intercessory prayer because it can see a bit of the future and the direction toward which things are moving.

This kind of prayer does not thrive with scheduling or planning. It just happens. We can create space for it by making sure our schedules aren't so hectic that all silence is squeezed out. We can go for a walk, sit and listen to quiet music, or wake up 15 minutes early in order to make a place for introverted intuitive prayer to happen.

Intuitive prayer, particularly introverted intuitive prayer, is often considered to be true prayer—mystical and contemplative. We must always affirm that it is one kind of prayer only.

Extraverted Thinking Prayer

"O, Lord, God of Abraham, Isaac, and Israel, let it be known this day that you are God in Israel, that I am your servant, and that I have done all these things at your bidding. Answer me, O Lord, answer me, so that this people may know that you, O Lord, are God" (1 Kings 18:36, 37).

Extraverted thinking is a process of analysis and decisionmaking based on logic, with application in the outer world. When we use extraverted thinking in prayer, we take the truth of God and apply it to the outer world. This kind of prayer involves a lot of thinking and questioning, leading to the creation of structures and plans.

Extraverted thinking is extremely goal-oriented. For a Christian using extraverted thinking, the goals grow out of an understanding of God's truth. Extraverted thinking prayer can begin with Bible study, analyzing God's truth with an eye to application. This kind of prayer longs to apply God's truth in the areas of integrity, responsibility, justice, righteousness, and freedom. What structures make these ideals possible? What programs should our church establish? How can we make God's truth more visible in the world?

And what about our own lives? In extraverted thinking prayer, God meets us face to face with demands on our own lives in these areas. Extraverted thinking prayer is confrontational. In it we experience God's call to justice and ethical action.

This process of studying God's truth and then seeking to apply it is a form of prayer. It takes a leap for many of us to consider this process as prayer. Yet many who have preferences for thinking can experience a sense of disenfranchisement when intuitive or feeling types talk about their intimate experiences of God's presence. We must grow in affirming that the process of analysis in the light of God's truth can be prayer.

Other aspects of extraverted thinking prayer look more like conventional prayer. Using extraverted thinking prayer, we may pray deeply passionate prayers for justice in the world. We may be very concerned about personal disobedience in a friend's life, and we may be able to pray effectively that the person would obey God's truth. We may spend significant amounts of time praying for the implementation of programs and plans, because we see so clearly that the plans and programs have grown out of a concern for God's truth and priorities.

Writing prayers can be very helpful when we want to develop extraverted thinking prayer. In it we take our thoughts into God's presence. Thoughts are organized into words, and writing down the words can provide the discipline and structure to be sure that our thoughts bring us into communication with God. Using the structure of prayers written by others can also help us grow in extraverted thinking prayer because we can enter into the thought processes of the person who wrote the prayer.

Analysis and structure in order to apply God's truth in the world—these are the keys to extraverted thinking prayer, a process of bringing our thoughts about truth into the presence of God. The church's ministry and mission wouldn't exist without this kind of prayer.

Introverted Thinking Prayer

"Their delight is in the law of the Lord, and on his law they meditate day and night. They are like trees planted by streams of water" (Psalm 1:2,3).

Introverted thinking is concerned with truth and all its subtleties and nuances, and with all the possible connected ideas and far-reaching implications. Bruce Duncan writes that you are engaged in introverted thinking prayer "when you love the Lord your God with all your mind, praying with your intellect, wrestling with a portion of Scripture as Jacob wrestled with God."[7]

We use introverted thinking prayer when we meditate on a portion of Scripture and explore the meaning of words and concepts, when we analyze the structure and the language, and when we ask countless questions about the purpose and application of the text. In fact, one of the signs of the presence of introverted thinking is lots of questions. It's very difficult for many people to affirm that prayer can be so full of questions. Those who have introverted thinking preferences often feel left out and unwelcome in congregations that affirm that faith is always composed of answers, not questions. Yet how can we find answers if we never ask questions?

Introverted thinking prayer can bring us face to face with God because of our honesty in asking questions. This kind of prayer is confrontational; we have questions and God answers us. Maybe the answers are not as frequent as we'd like, and maybe many more questions arise from every answer, but we need to be careful not to minimize the importance of the fact that questions can bring us right into God's presence. The last chapters of the book of Job are an excellent example of this, and almost 50 psalms contain cries of complaints and questions to God.

The book of Romans provides a different kind of example of the exploration of truth with all its implications. It is a logical presentation of truth, supported with Old Testament Scripture and subtle side arguments. In congregational settings where emotive connection with God is emphasized, it's important to affirm that the logical exploration of God's truth is a long-standing value and is intimately connected to this form of prayer.

Introverted thinking prayer can be deeply concerned with truth and justice. While extraverted thinking may pray about programs to encourage truth and justice, introverted thinking is more likely to meditate on and pray about the meaning of truth and justice and the failure of humans to measure up in those areas. These meditations, thoughts, and prayers can be a powerful call to confession.

Introverted thinking draws on themes of truth and justice, full of intellectual nuance and leading to myriad questions. This kind of prayer provides depth and helps to keep our faith from being shallow and superficial.

Extraverted Feeling Prayer

"The Lord is good to all, and his compassion is over all that he has made" (Psalm 145:9).

Extraverted feeling is all about connecting with other people in support, encouragement, compassion, warmth, loyalty, and faithfulness. In extraverted feeling prayer, we bring those characteristics into prayer, praying for and with people, and asking God for the very best for them.

When discussing thinking prayer, we said that it's important to view study, reflection, and analysis as forms of prayer. If that's true, then we also need to view as prayer the actions of extraverted feeling, such as words of encouragement and practical acts of caring. Extraverted feeling enables us to reflect, for example, Christ's personal care for individuals by seeing the best intentions of the heart, cheering on every good deed, and connecting with people in ways that support them and make them feel loved. Extraverted feeling enables us to show kindness in deed as well as in word. It may be helpful to regard these deeds and words as a form of prayer.

Extraverted feeling can also manifest itself in ways that look like traditional prayer. Extraverted feeling prayer lends itself particularly to prayer in groups or in pairs. This is the prayer of support for individuals and their needs, thanking God for successes and accomplishments and interceding for every kind of human weakness and crushing pain.

One aspect of healing prayer is extraverted feeling prayer. Whether we are praying for the healing of inner pain or the healing of the physical body, it is extraverted feeling that enables us to experience the powerful waves of compassion and sympathy that empower us to pray with strength and conviction. The tenderness of extraverted feeling makes the prayers gentle and appropriate. Extraverted feeling enables us to care deeply about what happens to the other person and to pray in response.

Extraverted feeling prayer also allows us to connect with God in an emotive, heartfelt way. Extraverted feeling fuels prayers of praise that reflect intimacy with God, gratitude for our Shepherd's tender care, and a deep heart-connection with our Creator. This is prayer of immense gratitude for all God's gifts—physical, spiritual, and emotional. This is prayer of deep trust, in which we put ourselves into God's hands, picturing God enfolding our lives and carrying us.

The Bible's relational images will be particularly helpful in this kind of prayer: God as the mother who teaches the toddler to walk, Jesus as shepherd and friend, the Holy Spirit as comforter and companion in daily life. The way that Jesus describes his intimacy with the Father in John chapters 14 to 17 will be deeply meaningful when we experience extraverted feeling prayer, which is first and foremost a prayer of connections among people and connections between people and God.

Introverted Feeling Prayer

"I will sing of loyalty and justice; to you, O Lord, I will sing" (Psalm 101:1).

At the core of introverted feeling are deeply held values. These values may be invisible to the world because they are introverted, but they shape connections with people and with God. These values call us to quiet, reflective prayer in which we wait expectantly for God to speak to us, as well as to passionate prayer for the needs of the world.

The values of introverted feeling are shaped within us, and they are uniquely individual. Some of the values we may find linked to introverted feeling are peace, justice, love, compassion, wholeness, and goodness. Holding these values as we look at the needs of the world can be a powerful call to prayer. In introverted feeling prayer we bring to God individuals and situations in which these values are sorely lacking. Even the word "value" is too sterile to describe this passionate desire that God's priorities be established on earth, that God's peace and justice flood our world, that God's compassion touch people in need.

In introverted feeling prayer we experience an emotive connection to God, a heartfelt desire to be one with God. This kind of prayer calls us to silence and listening, so that God can touch our hearts and speak to us. While extraverted feeling prayers of affective connection with God overflow with personal images and exuberant thankfulness, introverted feeling prayers of gratitude may involve quiet meditation on one image and may require waiting patiently for God to speak through that image. This process of centering and quieting ourselves in order to listen affirms that God alone is the center of our lives. It affirms our intimate dependence on God and our personal connection to God.

The silence of God in response to our listening prayer can be particularly upsetting when we are using introverted feeling. The saints and mystics throughout the ages affirm that persevering in spite of the silence is the best course. This is easy to say, but difficult to do.

Introverted feeling prayer can be nurtured by meditating on a short section of Scripture, with the goal of personalizing it and making it our own. Memorizing Scripture can be very helpful, enabling meditation without having to look at the Bible. Writing letter-prayers in a spiritual journal can help us to get in touch with those hidden, inner values and communicate them better to others.

Retreats, particularly those drawing on the contemplative tradition, will be attractive to us when we are growing in introverted feeling prayer. Guided meditation and silent prayer with an external structure provided at a retreat can be very helpful.

A deeply personal connection with God and a quietly passionate desire for God's kingdom on earth are the hallmarks of introverted feeling prayer.

Where Is the Holy Spirit?

The characteristics of prayer based on the eight functions above must be fueled and empowered by the Holy Spirit in order for effective prayer to take place. Just because a person has developed extraverted feeling skills doesn't mean he or she will automatically be able to pray effectively in the pattern of extraverted feeling prayer. The purpose in describing the eight prayer patterns is to provide us a vocabulary for the variety of prayer forms that people experience. We can consider these eight styles of prayer as we plan congregational prayer events.

Enabling the Whole Congregation to Pray

Keeping these eight patterns of prayer in mind as we plan prayer events and worship services can be a good way to help people pray in many styles and meet God in a variety of ways.

When structuring prayer times that focus on thankfulness, we can be sure that people have the opportunity to thank God for:

- The beauty of the physical world and for our bodies, health, and the ability to move and exercise (extraverted sensing).
- All that God has done in our congregation, in our community, and in individual lives (introverted sensing).
- The future possibilities for our congregation and our community, for hope, for vision, for purpose (extraverted intuition).
- Images and metaphors that make our faith alive: God as light, bread of life, living water, and so on (introverted intuition).
- The order and structure that make faith practical and real, for

denominations and church government and discipline (extraverted thinking).

- The fact that God has communicated truth to us and that we can question and wrestle with God's truth and God's law (introverted thinking).
- The relationships in our congregation and in our community that make faith real, and the community of love and harmony that enables us to glimpse God's love (extraverted feeling).
- The deep and abiding values that we embrace: the call to peace making, the call to love the poor, God's call to love each other even in conflict (introverted feeling).

These eight prayer patterns can help us provide a variety of settings and styles of prayer to enable people to pray using a variety of functions. Here are some suggestions:

- Make your worship space beautiful. If you meet in a theater or multipurpose space, use movable plants, banners, or other decorations (extraverted sensing).
- Devise a way for people to remember God's faithfulness in your congregation. Make a video or prepare a newsletter with stories about your congregation's history (introverted sensing).
- Allow personal stories in worship or some other setting, stories that describe God's work in someone's life (introverted sensing and extraverted feeling).
- Create settings for contemplative prayer, which allow time for people to meditate on God's work in their lives (introverted sensing), symbols and metaphors of faith (introverted intuition), God's law and truth (introverted thinking), and God's love and peace (introverted feeling).
- Create settings where people can wrestle with Scripture, discussing the hard issues and not skimming over the complexities (introverted thinking).
- Create settings where people can pray for the congregation and its ministries, expressing concern for vision and purpose (extraverted intuition) and praying for specific plans and programs (extraverted thinking).
- Use a prayer chain or prayer meetings where people's needs can be prayed for (extraverted feeling).

Type and Bible Study

Many of the same considerations about each of the eight functions can be applied to Bible study. When we lead or teach a Bible study, or when we encourage personal Bible study, we often emphasize patterns that reflect our own strengths and preferred ways of doing things. Reminding ourselves of the diversity of the people in our congregations will help us be motivated to teach in ways that draw on each of the type functions.

Just as in prayer, people may meet God through one of their less-preferred functions, so we need to be sure that we are providing ways to connect with the Scriptures that draw on all of the functions.

Lectio Divina

Lectio Divina (sacred reading) is a pattern of attentive, silent Scripture reading that dates back to the early centuries after Christ. It can be used very effectively in a group setting, with time for individual interaction with the text, followed by group sharing of what people experienced. It is also a wonderful method of personal Bible study, allowing for personal connection with God.

In *Prayer and Temperament*[8] the authors point out that the steps in *Lectio Divina* closely parallel the four type functions. Some of the patterns described above for prayer can be applied to each step in *Lectio Divina*.

Lectio, the first step, is the careful reading of a Scripture passage with attention to all the details. *Lectio* uses extraverted sensing to observe the specifics of the passage and introverted sensing to imagine the sights, smells, sounds, and feel of the situation described in the passage so we can put ourselves into it. In this step we read with our full attention. As we read, we watch for a word or short phrase that jumps out at us, that "shimmers."

Meditatio, the second step, draws on the thinking function to reflect on the insights received through *lectio*. This is a process of chewing or ruminating on the passage in order to find the beauty and goodness of God's truth. In *meditatio* we begin the process of applying God's truth to our lives. This step is cognitive, but beware of trying to force a meaning. This step embodies the thinking function at its best and involves considering, weighing, and analyzing, guided by grace and connected to our lives.

In *oratorio*, the third step, we move further into applying God's word to our lives by incorporating this Scripture into our hearts and by opening our hearts to God. In *oratorio* we use the feeling function to respond to God honestly and openly with "words, thoughts, desires, feelings, resolutions, decisions, commitments, dedications; or through sorrow for past failures; through gratitude, praise, petition."[9]

Oratorio can also include a listening component, as we listen for God to speak to our hearts through the passage and through our personal response.

Contemplatio, the fourth step, continues the process of listening for God to speak. We allow the Scripture to settle in our souls, and we may return to the word or short phrase that stood out in the first step. In *contemplatio* we may also listen for a metaphor or image that God wants us to receive from the passage. We listen for new perceptions or insights that have arisen from the previous three steps. This listening draws on the intuitive function because it is receptive, it is centered around metaphor and image, it is full of hope, and it embraces the overall message of the passage to us. In *contemplatio* we may receive a new infusion of peace, joy, and love which affirms our mystical connection with God.

Of course, instructions for *Lectio Divina* can be given without ever mentioning type. Understanding the role of the type functions in the four steps is helpful because it may enable us to explain each step more clearly.

Lectio Divina has been a significant pattern of meditative Bible study for centuries, allowing for connection with God in many different ways. When we see the connection between the type functions and the four steps in *Lectio Divina*, we can see why it is a discipline that enables us to connect with God using our whole selves.

Bible Classes and Personal Bible Study

We can consider each of the four functions when we lead Bible study groups, teach Bible classes, or prepare personal Bible study materials for people in our congregations. Again, this will allow for a variety of responses to Scripture and will allow participants to bring their whole selves to the study.

Here are suggestions for using the four functions in Bible study:

Sensing. Allow time for people to observe the details of the passage. Focus on what the passage says in its most direct meaning.

Intuition. What possibilities are inherent in the passage? What symbols, images, and metaphors are used? What is the connection between this passage and the ones before and after it? What is the meaning or purpose of this passage?

Thinking. What questions does the passage raise? Analyze the various pieces of information raised using sensing and intuition.

Feeling. What response to God does the passage evoke? Consider the values present in the information raised using sensing and intuition.

Inductive Bible Study

Some Bible study guides use the inductive method to draw participants into a passage. In contrast with topical studies or Bible surveys, inductive Bible study seeks to begin with a passage and draw conclusions based on the passage, with emphasis on the context of the passage. Inductive Bible study relies on a threefold pattern, asking participants to discuss the passage in three ways: observation, interpretation, and application. We can enrich that process by considering the ways the four functions are used in the three steps.

Observation (sensing).
- What details do you notice?
- What repeated words and phrases do you notice?
- What words need further definition?
- What sensory descriptions (smell, color, taste, touch) make the passage seem real to you?

Interpretation (intuition and thinking).
- What patterns do you observe in the repeated words and phrases?
- What details that you observed are most significant?

- What are the main themes of this passage?
- Which themes are most important?
- What images and metaphors come to mind in connection with this passage?
- What truth about God and people is communicated?
- What is the meaning of this passage?

Application (intuition and feeling).
- What does the truth of this passage mean to you personally?
- What impact could this passage have on your life?
- What does this passage teach you about relationships with others and with God?
- What do you want to do in response to this passage?

Praying from a Biblical Passage

In small group settings and in Bible classes, people often want to pray based on a passage, but find it difficult to know how to do that. Here are questions that can help group members respond to a biblical passage in prayer:

- Thank God for what you observed in the passage (sensing and feeling).
- Thank God for the images and metaphors connected with this passage (intuition and feeling).
- Thank God for the truth communicated in the passage (thinking).
- Does the passage evoke a call to confession in the area of relationships (feeling) or truth (thinking)? Offer prayers of confession.
- Does the passage call you to pray for yourself, for obedience to the truth of God's character (thinking), or for further growth in relationships with God or with others (feeling)? Offer prayers of supplication.

God's Presence in Prayer and Bible Study

Considering the patterns of prayer and study based on the type functions can give us confidence that we as congregational leaders are providing a variety of ways that people can meet God and experience God's presence. We don't know how or where people will meet God, but we do know that there are a variety of styles and patterns of prayer. Type can help us discern and understand those styles and patterns.

CHAPTER 5

Type and Spiritual Growth

"I learned about Myers-Briggs type at a seminar two years ago," Anna says. "I had the typical 'Aha!' experience, where I understood for the first time some of the differences between people. I talked about it with my husband for awhile after that seminar. Then last month, in a course I'm taking on spiritual direction, they presented the same basic information about type. Again, the differences between people were highlighted. I saw some of the participants having that same 'Aha!' experience I had two years ago. But I already understood the fundamentals of type.

"I want to know what comes next. Last month they didn't go any further than simply describing the differences between people. That's nice, but there must be more. If psychological type doesn't help us move on in our spiritual lives, then it is virtually useless."

Anna is right. Most of the time, the basics of type are taught in congregations. People gain understanding of the behavior of their spouse, their family and friends, their co-workers. They gain a language to describe differences among people. Having such a language is enormously important. But there is much more.

Understanding psychological type can help us grow in our spiritual lives in at least three ways. The first half of this chapter will explore these ways. These three patterns of spiritual growth can be personally helpful to Christians who want to move ahead in their spiritual lives. On the one hand, understanding the patterns helps us identify what God is doing in our lives. We can make choices to stretch ourselves when we understand the ways we can expect to grow spiritually based on our type. In addition, understanding these three growth pathways can help us work better with others because we may have a deeper understanding of what they are dealing with in their personal spiritual growth.

Understanding patterns of spiritual growth based on type can be helpful to those who engage in spiritual direction, pastoral care, and crisis counseling. Sometimes the spiritual caregiver can see right to the heart of the issue by taking psychological type into consideration.

First Path to Growth: Self-Acceptance

Most people, when they first learn about type, experience growth in self-acceptance. "Now I see that God made me this way" is a common response at type workshops. Self-acceptance is the first and most basic aspect of spiritual growth through understanding type.

John (ESFJ) grew up in a family of thinkers. He couldn't present lightning-fast arguments to defend his point of view in family discussions. Often, after a discussion was over, he still felt sure that he was right. Sometimes events later proved that he had been right. He felt awful, though, that he could never convince anyone of his viewpoint. He was sure that his family viewed him as stupid. He wondered if maybe they were right.

Later, as an adult, he experienced some of the same dynamics in his work environment. He tried to speak up in team meetings, but people seldom took his opinions seriously. He envied the people who could think quickly and speak persuasively. He wondered what was wrong with him and why people never took him seriously.

John attended a type workshop at his church. For the first time he had the language to describe the two decision-making processes—thinking and feeling. He understood that because thinkers tend to use linear logic, they are able to describe to others how they arrived at their decision. Thus they are often more convincing when they speak. John's sensing preference gave him lots of data to present in discussions, but he was always most concerned with harmony among the people around him, so he never felt that he presented the data in a convincing way.

At the type workshop his drive for harmony was validated for the first time in his life. He understood that this acute awareness of the feelings of those around him came from his preferred method of making decisions, and that this method of decisionmaking had the potential to be just as accurate as the linear logical approach he grew up with. He began to believe that his ability to care for people was a valuable asset. He gained a sense of peace in the way God had made him.

In the *Bulletin of Psychological Type,* a specialist and educator in eating disorders describes her counseling sessions with Geneen, a 19-year-old anorexic.[1] Geneen scored as an ISTJ when she took the Myers-Briggs Type Indicator. She had labored over each question, assessing and reassessing each response, because she was trying so hard to be the person she believed her parents wanted her to be. When the author of the article, Heidi Dalzell, presented to Geneen the type profile of an ISTJ, Geneen began sobbing. She told Dalzell that the type she had just described was what her parents had always wanted her to be. She had worked very hard to try to become that person.

Discussing type allowed Geneen to articulate for the first time her inner conflict over her parents' expectations. Geneen's true type is ENFJ. Her drive for harmony, related to her dominant function of extraverted feeling, caused her to try very hard to please her family. Discussing type helped Geneen begin to dismantle her persona, the mask we all assume to meet the expectations of others.

A Sense of Relief

The introvert who has always felt a little overwhelmed in our extraverted world, the person with a perceiving preference who often feels slightly disorganized and disheveled, the woman with a thinking preference, the man with a feeling preference, the sensing type working in a profession dominated by intuitives—all these people experience a kind of relief to hear their "weaknesses" described as normal, healthy behavior, each with its strengths and shortcomings.

This initial burst of self-acceptance is a wonderful experience. One of the greatest gifts of psychological type is the neutral vocabulary it uses to describe human differences. I need more time alone for reflection because I'm an introvert. My friend, an extravert, needs more time engaged in activities. Both are healthy and normal. Each of us needs to find the balance that works for us.

I wish self-acceptance were easy and clear-cut, a simple task that we could achieve once and for all. Instead, it is a journey which for many of us takes much or all of our lives. We find entangled in the issues around self-acceptance all kinds of expectations that we internalize. These expectations come from our families, our society, our employers, and our faith institutions. In addition, sin and self-deception entwine their way into our hearts, confusing everything.

The Ongoing Journey of Self-Acceptance

I first learned about type more than ten years ago, and it was wonderfully refreshing. I grew up as a dominant introverted intuitive in a family and society that valued extraversion and sensing. I was dreamy, spacy, messy, and out of touch with reality compared with my family. Type gave me the language to understand these differences and to rejoice in the gift of introverted intuition.

I began my journey toward self-acceptance by understanding that every trait, every personality characteristic, is in itself neutral—neither good nor bad. But these traits are like coins. They have two sides. The positive side of introverted intuition is that I am able to imagine things and plan things without writing down a word. I can write whole articles in my head, or plan programs, design publications, or solve problems. But the coin has a flip side. Because of my dominant introverted intuition, I am easily fatigued when dealing with the physical world. What is going on in my head is more real than the outside world.

I often don't notice spots on my clothing. One time I went to a speaking engagement and wore shoes that didn't match. But the very worst manifestation of this flip side of the coin was the time I backed out of the garage with the back car door open. When I heard the crunch of metal and glass, I knew that once again I'd been thinking about something else at a moment when I needed to focus on the physical world.

It wasn't sinful that I damaged my car. It was simply stupid and expensive! But it is also true that my weaknesses can lead me into sin. When I am overwhelmed and fatigued from dealing with the details of the outer world, I can become testy, irritable, and downright mean.

Our strengths can also lead us into sin. I find it easy to worry and catastrophize. This comes from the strong side of my introverted intuition which enables me to imagine things so very easily. My imagination leads me to bring up images of disasters. When I dwell on those possibilities rather than trust the love and care of God, I have allowed my great gift of imagination to lead me into sin. Self-acceptance based on type isn't blind approval of everything I do that reflects my type. I still need to identify and confess sin when necessary.

Other issues of self-acceptance are raised by my auxiliary and tertiary functions. I find my weaknesses in the area of sensing to be frustrating and embarrassing, but most of the time I can manage to ignore them. More visible are the issues raised by my auxiliary and tertiary functions.

As an INTJ, I am an introverted intuitive, with my intuition supported by thinking, my auxiliary function. (See Table 3 on page 17.) I meet the world with analysis and logic. My tertiary function, feeling, is fairly well developed. The skill of feeling, with its care for human need and drive for harmony, is much more accessible to me than is sensing. This is partly because it is my third function rather than my fourth.

Feeling is more developed in me than it might be in other INTJs for two additional reasons. One is that I am a woman. In our culture women are usually encouraged to develop feeling skills. In addition, the Christian circles in which I have developed as a person have valued extraverted feeling skills. I have worked very hard to develop extraverted feeling skills because I wanted to show Christian love through caring. Because of my passion for Christian ministry, I have tried hard to care for people with the kind of care that enables people to experience God's love. I want to give the kind of personal, empathetic care that I know reflects the ministry of Jesus on earth.

I am deeply committed to my calling as a pastor. Yet as an INTJ, my deepest gifts relate to strategy and design, not to pastoral care. When I come home from a ministry setting where I have given a lot of care to individuals, I am exhausted. I don't have any reserves left. My head hurts, my eyes burn, and I feel overwhelmed.

I find it easy to hate this part of myself. I chafe at my limits. As I lie in bed resting (with earplugs in and a pillow over my head) after an intense time with people, I always wonder what I did wrong. I feel guilty for being so tired. Over and over I need to remind myself that a short period of rest will refresh me, that this is simply a weak area for me, and that simply being tired doesn't mean I did something wrong.

Of course, there may be sin involved. Suppose I have become convinced that God desires that I shouldn't be involved in a certain situation. Maybe God has impressed this sense of direction in my heart during prayer, or perhaps a friend has confronted me and I have agreed reluctantly about God's guidance. But I go ahead anyway and continue my involvement in that area. In that case, my fatigue would be due to sin.

Or if I become compulsive in caring inappropriately for people, my fatigue would be due to sin. But in many instances, when I have tried to do what I believe is right and appropriate, I have simply run out of energy more quickly because I was using my less-preferred function.

John (ESFJ), whom I mentioned earlier, has a similar ongoing struggle of self-acceptance, but in different areas. When he first learned about type, he began to affirm that his feeling decisionmaking style had merit. He was able to affirm in a new way his ability to care for people.

But John's journey of self-acceptance continues. As an ESFJ, his dominant function is extraverted feeling. His auxiliary function is sensing. John is a college professor. He loves enabling individual students to learn. He excels at designing step-by-step, hands-on instructional modules, a skill that draws on his extraverted feeling (helping the individual) and his sensing (sequential, concrete tasks).

John receives criticism at the university for some of his teaching methods, and he still finds it extremely difficult to articulate a defense. His predominantly NT colleagues come at him with their thinking function, with criticism and analysis. It feels just like his family of origin.

Thinking is John's inferior function. With his commitment to harmony, he is deeply hurt by his colleagues' criticism. "Why can't I explain myself more clearly?" he wonders. "I try to tell them why I do things the way I do, and it's almost as if I haven't spoken at all. I know my teaching methods get results. The students love what I do. Why can't I convince my colleagues? What's wrong with me that they don't respect me?"

As an academic, John has worked hard at developing his thinking skills, but it is still a weak area for him, the flip side of the coin of his care for individuals and his true servant's heart.

John continues to pray about his ability to articulate his viewpoints to his colleagues. He continues to try to thank God for his strengths and to accept that he is growing—too slowly he feels!—in his weak areas. His faith is deeply affected by the lack of harmony in his work setting. He prays that this lack of harmony won't lead him into the sins of bitterness and gossip.

Type gives John some level of understanding of what is going on in these conflicts, and it challenges him to grow in accepting both his strengths and his weaknesses as gifts from God. This journey of self-acceptance will continue, sometimes intensely, sometimes less intensely, for many years.

In natural human development we will grow in our ability to use our less-preferred functions, but they will probably always cause us some degree of trouble. Understanding how and when to use each function and accepting our weaknesses in each one, will probably be a lifelong journey. For many of us, facing our limits is very difficult, but it is an important part of letting God be God in our lives and learning to live as finite creatures.

Type can help us by giving us a vocabulary to describe and observe what is happening. Type can help us experience the fact that our strengths and weaknesses are value-neutral; they are not good or bad. Strengths and weaknesses are simply different sides of the same coin.

In congregations, understanding these processes at work in our staff, leaders, and co-workers can give us gentleness and patience as we work with others.

Second Path to Growth: Learning to Use All Functions

In the book *From Image to Likeness*[2] one of the authors, Harold Grant, the director of a community of Catholic lay volunteers, proposes a theory of type development over life. He believes that we develop our dominant function from age 6 to 12, our auxiliary function from age 12 to 20, our tertiary function from age 20 to 35, and our inferior function from ages 35 to 50. After 50, we grow in our ability to integrate each of these four functions. Understanding this developmental process and learning to use all these functions is a second area of spiritual growth described by type. (See Table 3 on page 17 for a list of dominant, auxiliary, tertiary, and inferior functions for each type.)

Within the type community there is disagreement about one small aspect of this pattern of type development. Almost everyone agrees that the dominant function (sensing, intuition, feeling, or thinking) is used in the preferred attitude (extraversion or introversion), that the auxiliary function is used in the opposite attitude, and that the inferior function is also used in the less-preferred attitude. For example, an ESTJ has a dominant function—thinking—which is used in the extraverted attitude. The auxiliary function is introverted sensing, and the inferior function is introverted feeling.

The dispute is about the attitude (extraversion or introversion) of the tertiary function. Harold Grant believes that the tertiary function is used in the same attitude as the dominant. Carl Jung, in *Psychological Types*,[3] believed the opposite. Using the example of an ESTJ, the tertiary function—intuition—could be either extraverted (in Grant's view) or introverted (in Jung's view). If you look closely at Table 3 on page 17, you'll see that the attitude of the tertiary function is left blank because of this disagreement. Perhaps the best explanation is that the attitude of the tertiary function varies from one person to the next.

Many people report that Grant's scheme is helpful to them in understanding their personal development. My own life closely parallels Grant's formula. In elementary school I spent hours and hours reading fiction and daydreaming (introverted intuition). In my teens I discovered science, math, and debate, and at 19 I returned to the faith of my childhood because I became convinced of the truth of Christianity (extraverted thinking). In my 20s and early 30s, I was involved in a lot of Christian ministry, and I worked hard to develop empathetic listening skills (extraverted feeling), so during this time my life follows Jung's scheme and not Grant's. In my late 30s and early 40s, I began to write fiction, an activity which drew on my extraverted sensing skills as I strove to incorporate details into my writing to make it come alive.

Others find Grant's scheme less helpful because they don't see the pattern of their lives reflected as clearly as I do. Whether or not a person's growth fits Grant's pattern, an important principle remains: we will develop different functions over the course of our lives. As these functions develop, our dominant function becomes more effective because it is served and informed more thoroughly by the other functions. These other functions provide balance to the strength of the dominant function. The other functions may come into prominence at different times in our lives as we are developing them, and we grow in our ability to use each of the four functions appropriately when necessary. Over time, most people can see that their dominant function remains their strongest gift and skill.

Therefore, the goal of my personal growth from the point of view of type is that I may become more effective as an introverted intuitive, that with each passing year my introverted intuition may be better informed and supported by the other functions. This relates to spiritual growth as well. I desire to know and serve God with my introverted intuition in a mature and healthy way. The secondary goal is to learn to use my other functions—extraverted thinking, extraverted feeling, and extraverted sensing—appropriately and wisely in my Christian service and in my life of faith.

All Eight Functions

Grant's scheme raises another question, however: Where are the other four functions in our lives? I can see the pattern of the four functions laid out by Grant and Jung and others. Because I am an INTJ, those functions are introverted intuition, extraverted thinking, extraverted feeling, and extraverted sensing. But where are extraverted intuition, introverted thinking, introverted feeling, and introverted sensing?

The four authors of the Singer-Loomis Type Deployment Inventory[4] have asked the same question. They have written an inventory to measure each of the eight possible functions in our lives. They believe that our Myers-Briggs type doesn't necessarily lay out the order in which the eight functions are used in our lives. It is possible, they say, for an ESFJ to have something other than extraverted feeling as dominant, and maybe introverted thinking isn't that person's inferior function. And each of the eight functions appears in that person's life in different levels of strength and competence.

Therefore, the Singer-Loomis inventory measures separately each of the eight functions (sensing, intuition, thinking, and feeling; each in the two attitudes: introversion and extraversion), with the goal of growing in the ability to use each of the eight in appropriate ways.

The Singer-Loomis inventory breaks the deeply held assumption about type patterns—that the dominant and inferior functions are exact opposites. Whether or not we want to make that assumption, it is still useful to consider the role of each of the eight functions in our lives.

My dominant function is introverted intuition. Where is extraverted intuition in my life? I understand extraverted intuition to be a way of exploring possibilities in the outer world. It took me a long time to recognize the few times that I use extraverted intuition. I don't use it easily. It tires me out and makes me irritable.

My auxiliary function is extraverted thinking. In the same way, it took me a long time to come to appreciate introverted thinking, an interior process of constant decisionmaking based on truth and logic. I've been exploring this function. It confuses me.

My tertiary function is extraverted feeling. I can see it clearly in my life, but introverted feeling is more mysterious, another kind of interior process involving firmly held values and passions.

My inferior function is extraverted sensing. Oddly enough, I use introverted sensing a lot. For me, it is the most easily understood of these four functions that don't fit in the normally accepted scheme of functions.

The drive toward growth and development is built into our minds and souls, and it is normal and healthy that we would develop psychologically and spiritually in each of these eight areas. We benefit by understanding these eight functions because they provide patterns to watch for in our lives. We can notice the hand of God, guiding us to maturity.

In addition, we can make conscious choices to develop each of the eight areas. For example, we can choose to develop new prayer disciplines based on the patterns of prayer for each of the eight functions described in chapter 4. We can also explore recreational activities that draw on each of the eight functions.

Once we are fairly secure in our own type, we can experiment with each of the other16 types. That's one way of experimenting with each of the eight different functions. We can read descriptions of each type and experiment with living that way. It helps us move away from the rigidity and one-sidedness that says, "I'm this type, so I can't do that." We can embrace challenge and growth and experiment with new patterns. In the end, we will become stronger and better informed as we use our preferred functions.

Third Path to Growth: Accessing the Shadow

According to Jung, our minds have two realms—the conscious and the unconscious. Our dominant function is entirely in the realm of the conscious mind. We use it with skill and we are usually aware of what we are doing, or we can become aware if we pay attention. Our auxiliary function, says Jung, is mostly in the conscious mind but partly in the unconscious. Our tertiary is only partly in the conscious mind, and our inferior function is mostly in the unconscious mind, with just a little of it in the conscious.

In the unconscious dwells our shadow, that part of our mind that contains our unfulfilled potential along with all the emotions, skills, and desires we have had to set aside during our lives. Because the inferior function is located mostly in the unconscious, the inferior can be a gateway to our shadow. This can be an exhilarating area of spiritual growth. It can also be scary, humiliating, and painful.

Our inferior function often reflects our areas of incompetence. I am still ashamed of that day when I drove my car out of the garage with the back door open. Because my inferior function is extraverted sensing, I have a very hard time staying in touch with the physical world, and my gross errors expose my ineptitude. Surprise, surprise! I am not God. I am finite. I am limited. I screw up. I cannot maintain the myth that I am good at everything. I really do need God.

We can be grateful for these limits because they put us in our proper place. Type can give us language to help understand what is happening.

But these areas of incompetence go deeper. In *Beside Ourselves: Our Hidden Personalities in Everyday Life,*[5] clinical psychologist Naomi Quenk describes the state of "being in the grip" of the inferior function. We become obsessed, emotional, irrational, and out of control when our inferior functions emerge under stress or in the midst of fatigue. The ENFP may become obsessed with trivial details when the inferior function, introverted sensing, makes an unscheduled appearance. The ISTJ may become impulsive and obsessed with possible catastrophes when the inferior function, extraverted intuition, emerges.

Table 4

THE INFERIOR FUNCTION UNDER STRESS

Type	Inferior Function	What it may look like when it emerges under stress
ESTJ ENTJ	introverted feeling	hypersensitivity emotional outbursts
ESFJ ENFJ	introverted thinking	excessive criticism twisted logic
ESTP ESFP	introverted intuition	internal confusion grandiose visions
ENTP ENFP	introverted sensing	withdrawal and obsessiveness focus on the body
INTJ INFJ	extraverted sensing	overindulgence in sensual pleasure obsessive focus on external data
ISTJ ISFJ	extraverted intuition	impulsiveness catastrophizing
ISTP INTP	extraverted feeling	hypersensitivity to relationships being overly emotional
ISFP INFP	extraverted thinking	combative criticism impulsive action

Adapted from *Beside Ourselves: Our Hidden Personalities in Everyday Life* by Naomi L. Quenk (Palo Alto, Calif.: Consulting Psychologists Press, 1993).

In my 20s and 30s I struggled a great deal with overeating. It took me a long time to make the connection between my periods of compulsive eating and my inferior function, extraverted sensing. Extraverted sensing at its best is an enthusiastic, joyful embracing of sensory experience. When extraverted sensing emerges under stress as an inferior function, it shows itself as poorly developed and overly emotional, and it can involve many kinds of excess of sensation and impulsive behavior, such as excessive TV-watching, out-of-control shopping, or compulsive eating.

All kinds of emotions usually accompanied my periods of compulsive eating: sadness over choices made and opportunities lost, regret at past mistakes, self-flagellation for my limits. Until I reached midlife, I ignored these emotions by eating more. As I have faced these emotions, I have grown in faith in many unexpected ways. And I seldom eat compulsively any more.

The emergence of the inferior function in times of stress will raise many thoughts and feelings. They are easy to ignore, but these emotions can enable us to meet God in a profound way. First and foremost, our need for God is exposed. Being "in the grip" of the inferior function is a profound call to confession and humility. It is vivid evidence that sin's power reaches deep into our souls.

In addition, we can reflect on the emotions that are exposed in these moments. These feelings contain what I call "soul messages:" communications coming from deep inside us. When "in the grip," I commonly experience a powerful sense of loss, particularly the loss of past opportunities. Rather than bury that sense of loss under more food, I can bring that emotion into the light and ask myself questions: Are all those opportunities truly lost? Is there some component of those unfulfilled longings that I could pursue now or in the near future?

During periods of compulsive eating, I became obsessed with past mistakes. But human beings learn from mistakes. This is another kind of soul message: my inner self is trying to tell me what I could learn from those past mistakes. If I face this obsession with past mistakes honestly and forthrightly, I may be able to recognize that those specific mistakes have come to mind at this particular moment because I have something to learn from them.

Seeking spiritual growth through deeper understanding of the shadow and "in-the-grip" experiences is a messy affair. There are no prescriptions or formulas. But God can use insight from these experiences to lead us to fullness of life. Jesus called the little children to him, and he said that we have to become like children in order to inherit the kingdom of God (Matt. 18:3). There is nothing like incompetence or obsessions to show us that we are like little children, in need of God's care!

Learning to allow the inferior function to teach us some of the unfulfilled potential that lies hidden in our unconscious minds is a process of prayer, reflection, and talking. Most of us cannot do this work alone. We need spiritual friends and mentors. In order to process and understand this part of our spiritual growth, a spiritual director, pastoral caregiver, or a good friend will probably be essential.

In congregations we need to come alongside each other with patience and gentleness, giving each other affirmation and support as we face up to the excesses and immaturity that are exposed when our inferior function emerges under stress. When our co-workers and friends are negative and overwhelmed, we can listen carefully. We can also gently ask about the unfulfilled potentials that may be revealed through this emergence of the inferior function.

The Special Challenges of Midlife

Harold Grant's scheme of type development raises some fascinating questions about spiritual development at midlife. If it is true that most of us are growing in competence to use our inferior functions between the ages of 35 and 50, and if it is true that the inferior function often acts as an admission ticket to some of the shadow material in our unconscious mind, and if the shadow includes our unfulfilled potential, then we would expect the midlife years to be a rich and challenging time in our spiritual lives, a time of growing in integration and wholeness. This is often true.

It is also true that midlife can be confusing and disorienting, a messy time that makes people feel that they are unwelcome in the faith community. Some psychologists say that one of the tasks of midlife is to unpack some of the material in the shadow—the dreams, aspirations, hopes, and desires we set aside at various times of our lives for the sake of the needs that were present at those times. As those unfulfilled potentials come to the surface, we may be filled with regret and deep pain at the choices we made. In the midst of the "niceness" of life in congregations, it often feels as though deep pain is not welcome.

As midlife draws us into new tasks, we may find our competence level drops a little. Let's consider Bob, the INFJ mentioned in an earlier chapter, who has taken on the task of organizing the ushers. He begins with this ST organizational task, drawing on his less-preferred functions. He finds himself feeling rather pleased to undertake a task so straightforwardly. As he makes calls to set up the schedule, he listens with his customary insight and care to the people he talks with. He discovers that many of the ushers are upset about a change in the worship pattern, a change initiated by the pastor without any input from anyone and which slights the role of the ushers.

The usher-scheduling falls aside as Bob cares for the people he listens to. He is concerned for them as individuals, but he is also concerned about the way the pastor makes decisions. He finds himself unable to complete the concrete task of scheduling the ushers on time because he falls back into his preferred functions—intuition and feeling—which call him primarily into exploring possibilities for people.

At midlife people may take on tasks related to their less-preferred functions, tasks which they believe they can complete; but circumstances call them back to their more preferred functions. Then these new tasks don't get done very well.

It is vitally important in congregations that we affirm people's choices of where to serve, even when it seems to us that they may not do a great job fulfilling their responsibilities. Without new challenges, we can't grow, and growth and change are a significant part of human development.

The drive to use the less-preferred functions can have other unsettling aspects as well. Susan is an ESFJ whose calm, servant heart has been a mainstay to the women's ministries at her church for many years. At midlife Susan is drawn to use her less-preferred functions—intuition and thinking. This call isn't conscious or planned. Susan simply finds herself asking questions she never asked before.

Susan has volunteered from time to time at a battered women's shelter. Always before, she was grateful to be able to help these women in need, in small practical ways. Now she finds herself asking questions about the patterns of domestic violence. She reads everything she can find about police policies. She also comes across articles describing the role of Christian churches in supporting domestic violence.

She continues to be involved in the women's ministry at her church, but more often her major topic of conversation is domestic violence. She is angry and strident when she gets onto the topic. The other women, equally saddened by violence against women, don't know how to cope with Susan's intensity. When she begins a tirade against the church, the other women are baffled and confused.

Someone whose preferred functions are intuition and thinking has had most of a lifetime to develop the skills of seeing the big picture and being concerned with justice. Certainly, NTs can become strident and intense, but in general they are able to use their analytical abilities in a mature fashion. Someone who has spent a lifetime using sensing and feeling will not be able to use intuition and thinking as maturely. In Susan's case, intuition and thinking are often childlike and overly emotional. No wonder the other women are uncomfortable when Susan expresses her NT convictions.

Susan needs pastoral care, a spiritual director, or an insightful friend to help her navigate the intensity of what she is experiencing at midlife. She is puzzled by the passion of her convictions. She dislikes making the people around her feel uncomfortable, but she is captured by the issue of domestic violence. She can't let it go.

As leaders, we need to grow in tolerance for the messiness of midlife. Type can help us understand what is going on. Midlife provides a wonderful challenge to faith communities to address issues of meaning and values that are right at the core of our faith. In *Navigating Midlife: Using Typology as a Guide,* counselors and consultants Eleanor S. Corlett and Nancy B. Millner write that at midlife people often find themselves pulled two ways,

> concerned with matters of everyday, practical importance on the one hand, and with matters of meaning and purpose on the other. People experiencing midlife often ask themselves not only *how* they are able to live, but *why*, a question that points to the very meaning of their lives.[6]

Corlett and Millner go on to say that midlife is a time of developing new spiritual values. The church needs to develop a tolerance for the messiness of midlife in order to come alongside people as they walk through this stage of life. Significant faith issues are at stake.

Congregations need to do a better job of articulating some of the

Type can be useful for directees who are at midlife, because at that time many people experience a call to use the less-preferred functions in new ways. Type can provide a useful vocabulary to describe what is happening.

When helping a directee grow in prayer, a spiritual director may want to use the eight patterns of prayer described in chapter 4 as a guideline to lay out new directions in prayer. Directees can identify the prayer patterns they have used most frequently, and the director can make assignments for prayer exercises based on least-preferred functions.

It is very helpful for the director to consider the type development going on in the directee's life. It is equally important for spiritual directors to consider their own type as they engage in this ministry. Almost every type needs to be careful of their natural tendencies that can get in the way of effective spiritual direction.

- Extraverts need to be careful not to talk too much. Listening is the central skill of spiritual direction.
- Introverted intuitives need to be careful that they allow directees to discover God's hand in their lives themselves. Introverted intuitives often know very rapidly what the central issues in other people's lives are—or they think they know! Their ability to leap to a conclusion, even if it is often insightful, can get in the way of the kind of careful listening and quiet coming-alongside that spiritual direction requires.
- Extraverted intuitives need to be careful that they don't overwhelm directees with too many options or possibilities.
- Extraverted thinkers need to watch out for their tendency to problem solve. Practical assignments are often a part of spiritual direction, but practical solutions to spiritual issues must be suggested sparingly.
- Introverted thinkers need to limit analysis.

The Rev. Peter Malone, an Australian Catholic who trains spiritual directors, believes that all types can be effective spiritual directors if they understand their natural propensities to excess. He believes ISFJs are the most naturally gifted spiritual directors.[7] They often have a remarkable ability to listen. Their extraverted feeling enables them to be encouraging, and their sensing enables them to stay in the present with the directee, rather than making a leap into possibilities like an intuitive would do.

For those of us who are not ISFJs, this statement by Peter Malone can be a wonderful, positive challenge. As we engage in spiritual direction, we can practice the sensing skills of staying in the present and the feeling skills of giving encouragement and conveying acceptance. If part of growth is experimenting with and growing in our less-preferred functions, then spiritual direction provides many of us with an excellent opportunity to grow and develop.

Facilitating Spiritual Growth Based on Type

I am delighted that so many more traditions are embracing spiritual direction, because it is one practice that can be very helpful in promoting spiritual growth among individuals. Here are some other suggestions for facilitating spiritual growth based on type:

- Encourage congregational leaders to try new tasks, and encourage tolerance for some level of incompetence in achieving those tasks.
- Encourage leaders to take sabbaticals from service, particularly at midlife.
- Offer adult classes or seminars on the spiritual issues of midlife, including the type implications.
- Encourage members to try new prayer patterns based on all of the eight functions.
- In sermons and classes, talk about the fact that we are all growing, and that this means we must experiment with new things, which will probably be a bit messy.

Understanding patterns of spiritual growth, particularly growth in self-acceptance and growth through facing the inferior function and the shadow, can help us develop a spirit of gentleness and kindness as we work with others in our congregations. We are all growing. We are all "people in progress." We all experience stress and behave in childish ways when under pressure. We need a kind word or a gentle listening ear when we experience growth pangs. I long for our congregations to be places offering that kind of love and acceptance along with tolerance for the complexity of our spiritual journeys.

CHAPTER 6

Type and Congregational Activities

Teri has agreed to serve on the planning committee for the all-church retreat. She loves retreats, and she enthusiastically enters into the discussion about the highest priorities for this upcoming event.

"Let's plan lots of activities," she says. "A speaker, small groups, and lots of recreation and games. And let's make sure that everyone participates in everything. I love the feeling of a group of people being together all weekend."

Peter, another member of the committee, jumps in. "It's important to offer choices," he says in his quiet voice. "Lots of people have a busy workweek, and they need some quiet on a retreat weekend. Some people will want to rest during the recreation time. Or maybe take a hike alone."

"But I don't like that," Teri replies. "I like the whole group to be together all weekend. That really builds community. Somehow we have to communicate that the games and recreation aren't optional. We have to let people know that we expect them to be there."

"No, we don't," Peter replied. "Part of why I wanted to serve on this committee is because I wanted to ensure that there would be an option for down time during the weekend. Last year's retreat was too busy."

"We really built community last year," Teri argued. "It was just right."

"Not for me," Peter answered. "I came home exhausted."

Teri and Peter's discussion illustrates some of the challenges in planning congregational activities. Understanding type can help us plan to meet some of the diverse needs in our congregations.

Teri is probably an extravert and Peter is probably an introvert. But it's also slightly possible that Teri is an introvert who leads a very quiet life and enjoys the change of pace offered by a highly relational retreat. Peter might be an extravert who works at an extremely fast-paced job and looks for the balance of some quiet time during his weekends.

As we consider type in planning congregational activities, we must emphasize again that it is important not to believe, for example, that we offer quiet activities only for introverts and lots of interaction only for extraverts. We want to offer a variety of activities to meet needs in the areas of both extraversion and introversion, no matter who is experiencing those needs.

In this chapter we'll look at each of the four type preferences and explore options for programs that address the needs of both preferences.

Extraversion and Introversion

A few years ago I attended a one-day retreat that included a lovely balance of activities to facilitate expression of both introversion and extraversion. The day opened and closed with a five-minute period of reflection and silent prayer, with specific instructions regarding topics to consider during the five minutes. The bulk of the morning was a presentation by the pastor and his wife. The morning ended with small-group activities for a period of 45 minutes.

Because the weather was nice, people could eat their sack lunches in informal groups on the lawn. The afternoon began with a half-hour question-answer session with the pastor, based on the morning's topic. Then a layperson led an extended guided meditation. We were given 45 minutes alone, to write in our journals, think, or pray, with specific suggestions of topics to write about or think about. There was then more time in the same small groups, followed by an energetic wrap-up session for the whole group.

Several factors made the retreat comfortable for introverts and for extraverts who needed to use their introverted sides:

- opening and closing the retreat with five minutes to reflect and pray

- a block of 45 minutes to journal, walk around, or think

- assigned small groups, so that by the second session the members of the group were starting to get to know each other and be able to trust each other

- choices for lunch, so people could be with large or small groups as they wanted

Other factors enabled the extraverts (or the introverts who needed to use their extraverted side) to feel comfortable:

- the large group sessions conveyed a feeling of energy and unity

- specific suggestions for the times of silence and topics for writing or reflection kept the times of silence from seeming overwhelming

- the small groups provided an opportunity to think out loud about faith

If I had been helping to plan the event, I might have been tempted to say, "The introverts will get their time alone at home anyway, and the extraverts won't like it, so maybe we shouldn't 'waste' that time during the retreat." However, in my own small group, three people mentioned that their lives are so busy that there is no time for reflection. One woman said, "I know God must be active in my life. But it takes time to reflect on my life to see the way God is working, and I simply never take that time. It's been nice today to have that time structured in."

It's important to consider which activities will appeal to introverts and to schedule them in, so that busy people—introverts as well as extraverts—will have some time for reflection. As the pace of modern life continues to speed up, providing reflective experiences in congregational events will continue to be fruitful for many participants.

Adult Classes

Some of the same ideas can be applied to adult classes. When I teach adult classes at church, I've recently begun leaving a two- to three-minute period of silence at the end. I suggest to the class members that they use the time to consider what they would like to take home from the class to apply in their daily lives.

Somewhere, a long time ago, I heard it said that we remember a much higher percentage of what we say than what we hear. Because of that idea, I tried for many years to teach classes almost entirely by discussion. I have recently changed that practice. As an introvert, I find it exhausting to teach totally by discussion. Teaching by discussion requires connecting with a class by using extraverted functions that require effort: extraverted feeling to connect relationally with the people who contribute an idea, extraverted intuition to discuss the big-picture possibilities, extraverted thinking to analyze and respond to ideas that are presented, and extraverted sensing to observe the details in what people say. Some of these functions are relatively easy for me to use, such as extraverted thinking (my auxiliary function), but the others are quite a drain.

Lecturing, on the other hand, is less draining because I can plan what I want to say ahead of time in my head. I now use a combination of lecture and discussion. I changed my practice because of my own needs.

Later I found out that lecture can be an effective means of teaching introverts. They usually work with their own thoughts; therefore, reflecting on what they hear in a lecture can be an effective way to learn. I see now that a certain amount of lecturing in a class provides me—and the other introverts—with a break from interaction. Yet I still affirm the benefits of a certain amount of discussion to enable class participants to interact with the material.

When we are conducting classroom discussions, it's important to pause occasionally and say, "Is there anyone who hasn't spoken who would like to?" We need to do this to honor the communication style of introverts, who often think deeply before they speak. At the same time, there is no need, from the standpoint of facilitating learning, to force people to share by going around the room and asking everyone to speak. Gordon Lawrence, in *Looking at Type and Learning Styles,* writes, "Research shows that the quality of students' learning in classroom dialogue has nothing to do with how often they speak or whether they speak at all."[1] We may choose, once in awhile, to circle the room in order to have everyone share on some particular topic, but we do not need to do so because we are afraid the silent ones are not learning anything.

Lawrence affirms that generally introverts prefer to extravert when they choose to; usually they don't appreciate being forced to do so. He says introverts benefit from being given advance warning of expectations to extravert. They usually appreciate having time to prepare what they will say or do.

Lawrence believes that extraverts learn well in small groups and with partners, where they can think out loud. He suggests that extraverts benefit from projects that involve talking, such as "interviewing, oral histories, conducting surveys, contacting resource people, performing, displaying, orally explaining, and demonstrating."[2] Incorporating some of these activities into adult classes would be an excellent way to engage extraverts.

Extraverts usually prefer to act first and reflect later. Introverts prefer to reflect first and act later. These seem like totally incompatible patterns, but there are classroom activities that work for both. Manuscript Bible study is one example.

The manuscript method of Bible study was pioneered several decades ago by InterVarsity Christian Fellowship. A book of the Bible, or a section of a biblical book, is typed double-spaced on standard size paper with generous margins, then photocopied for each participant. In a classroom setting, with participants sitting around tables, the time would be roughly divided into thirds. The first third is individual study. Participants are encouraged to mark up their manuscripts, usually one to three pages in a class session, using colored pens or pencils. They can underline or circle repeated words and ideas. They can draw lines that connect those repeated words. They can mark blocks of text. Some devotees of this method actually tape all the pages together so they can draw lines from one page to the next.

In the middle third of the class time, class members discuss the passage in small groups, usually without a leader. Participants are asked to describe what they noticed as they studied individually. In the last third of the class, the teacher moderates a large group discussion, trying to draw together the themes and ideas discussed in the small groups and trying to encourage application of the truths in the text.

Extraverts usually enjoy jumping into a task and doing something. That first activity in manuscript Bible study allows them to dive into the text, wielding a variety of colored pens and highlighters. It usually feels to extraverts that they are definitely doing something fun as they mark up the pages of the biblical text.

Introverts usually enjoy reflecting before they talk. Manuscript Bible study allows them the opportunity to study the passage quietly before they are expected to discuss it. The pattern of study in manuscript Bible study illustrates that having a specific task to do at the beginning of a class, one that can be done alone but that involves some activity, can minister to both introverts and extraverts.

Small Groups

Small groups are one fellowship setting that provides an ideal structure for both introverts and extraverts. Tom, an extravert, has been in the same men's group for eight years. He says, "I'm so grateful that five other guys have set aside the time to help each other. I like hearing their ideas, what God is doing in their lives, what the Scriptures mean to them."

Tom says the Bible study component gives him a chance to think out loud about what he finds in the Scriptures. "I'm thinking about issues even as I'm saying them. When I say something, I'm trying it on to see how it fits. It's not like I have an insight before I start talking."

Listen to the difference when Maury, an introvert, describes his experience in a small group. "My small group is the one church setting where people really listen to me. They draw me out and ask me questions about what I think and feel, about what I believe. It's one of the few places where we go deeper, where we leave superficial chitchat behind and get to the real meat of the Christian faith."

Many of the books integrating type with Christian faith say that extraverts will enjoy large and small groups, while introverts will enjoy journaling, silent prayer, and prayer partnerships. In contrast to this view, I have found that many introverts are quite enthusiastic about small groups in which they can get to know the members and feel safe sharing their thoughts, reflections, and feelings.

It's easy to assume that introverts usually prefer to be alone and extraverts usually want to be with people, but Jung didn't define introversion and extraversion that way. Introverts commonly need more time to reflect, but they also need and enjoy relationships, particularly if they feel safe enough to share their reflections. Most introverts need to know that their confidences and ideas will be treated with respect. An ongoing, small group is an ideal setting for the type of sharing that will be respected.

Extraverts usually enjoy small groups because they provide a place to process out loud and to share their lives. A small group at a retreat, gathered together for a one-time event, will usually appeal more to extraverts than to introverts. The effort to meet new people may fatigue the introverts, and they will seldom feel safe enough to share deeply during their first gathering with a group. But if the same group gathers for a second or third time over the course of a weekend and an atmosphere of trust is established, many introverts will begin to feel free to share.

Meetings

Extraverts are more likely than introverts to find meetings enjoyable, because they are more likely to enjoy conversing with others, discussing a topic, and bringing options into the open. I am one introvert who finds meetings very tiring. Sometimes I think the biggest service that can be provided to introverts is to keep meetings as short as possible. Many tasks can be accomplished by phone conversations and e-mail. The rapid pace and sheer overload experienced by so many parishioners will necessitate fewer committee meetings in the future, and, as an introvert, I think that's great.

Introvert-extravert issues in meetings begin before the meeting ever starts. Introverts usually like to think about things before they talk about them, so introverts will usually appreciate notes or a written agenda before the meeting takes place. In the absence of written information, a phone call listing the major topics of the meeting will usually help introverts be prepared for discussion.

The major introvert-extravert issues in meetings revolve around who talks and how much. As a very talkative introvert, I know that there are quiet extraverts and chatty introverts, so some of the advice for enabling introverts to share will also apply to quiet extraverts. During a meeting, when an issue has been discussed for awhile it is helpful to introverts for the chairperson to say, "I'd like to offer the opportunity for those who haven't said anything on this topic to speak." Expect some silence before the introverts dive in! Often it will be well worth waiting for, because the introverts may have been thinking deeply on the topic while the others were talking.

Extraverts need the opportunity to think out loud at meetings. Often introverts only talk about their ideas after the ideas are fully formed, so introverts can find it difficult to understand that an extravert is often forming an idea while speaking. The introvert thinks, "He plans to implement that idea," while the extravert is thinking, "This is one way of doing the task." This can cause misunderstandings.

One Presbyterian pastor, at the end of every session meeting, goes around the room and gives each person the opportunity for a closing comment. Each elder can pass, so there is no pressure to speak, which is helpful for the introverts.

Allowing this opportunity for closing comments ministers to introverts who may have been thinking about something throughout the meeting but just couldn't figure out how to break into the discussion. This opportunity also ministers to the extraverts who may also need to say one more thing. The pastor says this practice helps to avoid parking-lot meetings after the official meeting ends, which in turn reduces factions and dissent.

Worship

In order to minister to the introversion and extraversion needs in all of us, worship services need to have some blend of quiet, introspective moments along with times full of energy, enthusiasm, and connection with people.

Opportunities for silence include:

- a moment of silence before the introit or call to worship

- silent confession of sin

- a period of silence during intercessory prayers when the congregation is instructed to pray for something specific, such as "missionaries you know," "people in your life who need God's touch," or "your own personal concerns"

- the traditional prayer of *examen* may be used, in which the congregation is asked to remember the places in the past week in which God acted in their lives.

For most congregations one or two periods of silence in a service are enough. The silences need to be long enough—30 seconds to two minutes—to allow people to pray. I become intensely irritated when silent prayer is broken off after five seconds.

In addition to silence, a service can minister to the introversion needs in all of us by having periods when the pace is slow and unhurried.

Opportunities for high energy and enthusiasm include:

- announcements, perhaps with skits or jokes
- peppy music
- children's sermons
- the sermon

It would be useful to sit down with a group of introverts and extraverts and ask them to evaluate your worship services. It will probably be striking that one person loves the exact thing that another person hates. That's why variety is so important.

Preaching

Issues of introversion and extraversion affect the content of sermons more than they do the style. Introverts are often more concerned about individual spirituality and enabling a personal connection with God, while extraverts are often more concerned with action and behavior.

If you are an introvert who preaches, and if you are particularly motivated in the area of personal spirituality, be sure your sermons provide some emphasis on spirituality in action. Consider questions of relationships, service, and obedient behavior.

If you are an extravert who preaches, be sure that you bring personal spirituality into your sermons. From time to time, discuss personal devotions and personal experience of God. Validate prayer as a significant ministry in your congregation.

Sensing and Intuition

When we are using our sensing function, we are usually concerned with practical issues that have an impact in the present. When we are using intuition, we are usually concerned with the big-picture issues of purpose and meaning. These two priorities often collide in church programs. Yet when both issues are addressed, church activities have a richness and wholeness that is very attractive.

Worship

In one church, the worship committee evaluated the worship service and discovered that many of the activities of their typical service ministered to the intuitive side. The sermon was a major part of the worship, and the pastor, a dominant intuitive, loved to preach about issues of meaning, using metaphors and images. The worship often centered around a theme and was highly conceptual.

The committee believed that the majority of the congregation preferred sensing and that the majority of people in the neighborhood also preferred sensing. They set out to bring a sensing component to their worship.

They began with banners and seasonal flowers, neither of which had been used before. They brought in a drama group for one service, which encouraged some teens to form an ongoing drama group for worship. For stewardship Sunday they asked congregation members to write a prayer for their church. Each person walked to the front of the church and put both the prayer and a pledge card into a basket. The prayers and pledge cards were dedicated in the service. This physical expression—the act of writing on a piece of paper and carrying it forward—addresses sensing needs.

On Good Friday a large wooden cross was brought into the church. Each person was invited to write his or her burdens on a piece of paper. Nails and hammers were provided to hammer the papers to the cross. On Easter the same cross was covered with chicken wire, and worshippers were given flowers to twine in the chicken wire, producing a beautiful cross of flowers.

All of these new activities had sensing components which enabled the congregation to express that part of their lives in worship.

After some analysis, a congregation may find that its worship service has a dominant sensing flavor. Such a service might be characterized by an order of worship that is always carefully followed to the letter, lots of detail communicated through announcements, sermons that are very practical, and prayers that focus on concrete needs. That congregation may wish to consider ways to enrich its service by bringing metaphors and verbal images into the prayers and sermons, by centering the services around a theme, and by varying the order of worship to fit that theme. Statements of purpose address intuitive needs: "We are here today in worship because we recognize our need for God and we want to draw near our loving Creator."

Creature Comforts and the Big Picture

When intuitives–which includes many pastors–teach classes and run congregational programs, they need help to remember to attend to the participants' physical needs.

- Is the room comfortable? Consider the comfort and arrangement of the furniture, the temperature, and the noise from outside.

- Is the lighting adequate? This a particular concern for aging people. The light available in many church classrooms and meeting rooms is inadequate for the needs of people's eyes as they get older.

- Is there something attractive about the room, maybe a small bouquet or an interesting poster?

- Are the handouts somewhat attractive, or are they tenth-genera tion photocopies that are ugly and hard to read? In this day of computer graphics and desktop publishing, it is completely unnecessary to use boring, unattractive handouts.

- Are coffee and tea available?

If people who prefer sensing are running a program, they need to remember that people who prefer intuition usually need to know why something is happening and what the purpose or goal of the event is. Intuitives usually need to be assured that they are not expected to "go through the motions."

A simple statement of purpose at an event's beginning will go a long way to address that intuitive need. "We're here at this lunch today to get to know each other better and to raise money for the church's tutoring program." "This committee is charged with overseeing the stewardship program. Our goal is that each person in the congregation be encouraged to be a good steward of time and money. We have to talk about a lot of nuts and bolts tonight, but let's not lose sight of our purpose."

In the Classroom

Someone with a preference for sensing will usually desire practical lessons in the classroom, while an intuitive will usually be motivated by inspiration—something that sparks the imagination. An effective teacher will combine overview and big-picture issues (intuition) with practical and concrete application (sensing).

Hands-on materials can help sensors connect and learn, while intuitives often enjoy learning through the power of words—metaphors, images, and abstraction. Classes that incorporate both aspects will help all people learn.

In Bible study discussions it is particularly important to get to application. Leaving out application can kill the effectiveness of the Bible study for the sensing types present. Interesting points about God, intriguing images that capture the imagination, and the purpose of the passage—which intuitives will enjoy as ends in themselves—will not be enough for most people with sensing preferences. They will want to know what difference the passage could and should make in their lives.

Intuitives will probably not enjoy application questions that are dogmatic or rigid. An intuitive may respond best to open-ended application questions that include options such as "What are some possible practical applications of this passage?" or "What do you think you might want to take home from this passage for your everyday life?"

The Building and Institutional Memory

Congregational leaders who prefer intuition are likely to be concerned with the congregation's faithfulness to its purpose as a faith community. For example, a Christian leader would ask: Is the church bringing forth the kingdom of God on earth? Is it showing Christ's love, compassion, truth, and justice? Is it working for peace in the world? Is it spreading the Gospel?

If a congregation has many intuitive leaders and members, there is a very real danger they may neglect the building. After all, the larger issues of faith are more important than bricks and mortar.

There is an equal danger that the congregation's record-keeping may be sloppy. This can have an impact on financial matters and institutional memory. Does the congregation have some sense of its history? Are records of past decisions available for easy consultation? Do leaders seek wisdom in earlier decisions? Reinventing the wheel can be a drain on resources. Intuitives–including many pastors–can have the tendency to do just that because they find the details of record-keeping boring.

If a congregation has many people with sensing preferences, the building and grounds may be immaculate, the history may be recorded on videotape, and all the finances may be in excellent order. This sensing preference needs the balance of continual reminders of the overall purpose. In the short run, people with sensing preferences will be content to keep things in order, but in the long run they need the balance of the kind of vision and inspiration intuition prompts.

Preaching

We need to be particularly careful to address issues of sensing and intuition in sermons, because sermons without a strong dose of both can be unbalanced and ineffective.

The intuitive preacher is likely to omit the kind of sensing details that bring life to stories. One way to check for sensing details is to see if the five senses are mentioned somewhere in each sermon. Another way is to look over each illustration in the sermon. Is it well-written like an effective short story? Does it include enough sensing detail to bring the listeners into the story?

The sensing preacher may tend to forget the big picture and neglect the lofty themes. Can you state the main point of your sermon? Can you relate the main point of the sermon to a major doctrine? What part of the Good News are you trying to communicate in this sermon?

The sensing preacher may also neglect the richness of biblical image and metaphor that enables us to meet God with our intuitive side. The sensing preacher may be uncomfortable preaching on texts that are full of image rather than linear logic. For the sake of the congregation's spiritual growth, it is important not to neglect the Bible's vivid verbal pictures.

Thinking and Feeling

In *Looking at Type and Spirituality,* Sandra Krebs Hirsh and Jane A. G. Kise vividly describe the impact of the thinking and feeling preferences on the practice of faith. They write that thinking involves "experiencing God intellectually."[3] Skepticism often precedes conviction. This intellectual approach will motivate people to get in touch with universal principles to guide faith. Debate and dialogue will be valued. Logical questions will be considered. Spiritual practices will be evaluated analytically.

Feeling, according to Hirsh and Kise, involves "experiencing God wholeheartedly."[4] Personal values will guide faith, and believers will search for personal meaning in studying the Bible. Conviction is supported by concerns for personal relationships between God and people. Inquiry and learning will arise from the study of motivations, inspirations, and examples of people's lives. Spiritual practices will be evaluated by their impact on people or on the community as a whole.

These different approaches to faith will have a great impact on relationships throughout the life of any congregation. As we have seen in preceding chapters, the potential for misunderstanding and hurt in this arena is significant. When we're discussing thinking and feeling differences, the central issues are mostly relational, and the patterns of scheduling and planning events aren't as significant as they are with the other type preferences. Considering issues of thinking and feeling reminds us over and over that as we interact interpersonally we need continually to grow in accepting and affirming the different faith convictions that grow out of these different preferences.

The person with a feeling preference will often care most that this person or this group of people be empowered or feel loved and accepted. The feeling person will usually not object to efficiently run programs or intriguing intellectual discussions, as long as the people needs are met first.

The person with the thinking preference is more likely to care about excellence in programming and/or high caliber intellectual stimulation. Thinking types will not object to programs that meet a person's need for affection, acceptance, and empowerment, but they are less likely to see those personal needs as the highest consideration.

These differences will affect discussions in every possible congregational setting, such as meetings, classes, and small groups. Careful listening and tolerance for different viewpoints are essential.

In the Classroom

Learning styles are heavily influenced by thinking and feeling preferences. Therefore, the classroom is one arena where we can benefit from considering thinking and feeling differences.

If the thinking preference usually manifests itself with an interest in the intellectual questions of faith, and if the feeling preference is usually more concerned with personal meaning and values, then lesson plans and teaching methods need to be tailored to both these preferences.

Gordon Lawrence writes that people with thinking preferences, particularly those with thinking as their dominant function, come to class looking for logically organized experiences. They want to learn cause-and-effect relationships. If they don't find logical reasoning, order, objectivity, and fairness, they will be frustrated.

On the other hand, Lawrence writes that people with feeling preferences, particularly those with feeling as their dominant function, look for a teacher who cares for students and who connects with the class with warmth and compassion. They want learning experiences they can put their heart into. They will experience stress if they find abrasiveness in the classroom, even if the abrasiveness is not directed at them personally.[5]

In congregational settings, as in all settings, teachers need to combine a warm communication style with rigorous intellectual exploration of the topic. Leaving out one or the other will greatly inhibit learning.

We can communicate warmth by smiling as we teach and by learning names and affirming people as they make contributions. Some people who teach frequently have told me they have greatly benefited from
having a host or hostess for each class who welcomes people, hands out
name tags, and makes sure tea or coffee is available. That frees the
teacher to focus a little more on the actual material being taught, while
still being committed to having a warm and welcoming classroom.

We can communicate our commitment to truth and intellectual inquiry first and foremost by welcoming questions. As the teacher, even as
a religious teacher, we don't have to give instant answers to all questions! We can refer the question to the class and ask for responses. We
can even ask, "What other questions does this question raise?"

Before the class starts, we can also work hard to construct our lesson plans with logic and thoroughness as a way of affirming our commitment to truth and intellectual inquiry.

Faith itself is excellent subject matter for classes that try to minister
to the thinking and feeling needs in all of us. Our faith embraces truth
and law, with a call to learn the principles of faith and to think hard
about what we believe. These address our needs to use our thinking function. Our faith also provides "subject matter to care deeply about,"[6]
which Gordon Lawrence recommends for people with a feeling preference. We want to learn about God's love and grace, and we want to
learn how to show God's compassion and caring in the world.

Indeed, it is much easier to embrace both thinking and feeling when
teaching classes in a congregation than in just about any other setting,
because of the nature of our faith.

Preaching

In a Christian setting, because the Christian faith has such a strong emphasis on both grace and truth, it will be fairly easy to include issues of
thinking and feeling in sermons. The preacher may find it useful to think
of a kind of checklist for each sermon:

- Does the sermon address issues of truth? Does it have logical
  structure and does it discuss issues in an analytical fashion? Does
  it have intellectual coherence? Are the listeners encouraged to
  think clearly? Does the sermon minister to the mind?

- Does the sermon address issues of human values? Are people and their concerns a focus of the sermon? Are the listeners encouraged to explore their personal convictions? Does the sermon minister to the heart?

Judging and Perceiving

Judging and perceiving describe one aspect of the way we conduct our lives in the outer world. When we prefer judging, we prefer to live our outer lives in a planful, structured fashion, and we desire closure in many areas. When we prefer perceiving, we'd rather live our outer lives with flexibility and openness.

I believe most congregations have a strong judging flavor. Services are carefully structured, and they begin and end on time. The belief system is laid out clearly in the creeds. Certain clothing is expected. Certain behavior is also expected, and when behavior violates expectations, repercussions occur. Even charismatic and Pentecostal churches, which may have more flexibility in their worship services, can be quite regimented with respect to beliefs and behavior.

None of this is inherently bad. However, we are in danger of forgetting that God is not inflexible; instead, as Bruce Duncan points out, God is "infinitely open, receptive and spontaneous. . . . never hasty . . . always 'slow to anger' . . . the God of delight and joy who laughs and plays and enjoys creation."[7]

The challenge is to provide enough structure to move forward as a congregation, but to retain enough flexibility to be open to the working of the spirit and to allow human diversity. We need goals and direction in order to be faithful to the call of God. We need structure and systems in order to meet goals. But there are limits to what structure can do. We need flexibility and openness in order to experience the full range of God's character as it is expressed through human beings.

In this era of embracing human diversity, the issues raised by the perceiving and judging functions are very real. How do we encourage diversity without abandoning the essential components of our faith? What are the limits of our call to accept diversity? Is it necessary to draw the line? How do we know where to draw it?

How can we strive to be flexible enough to respond to the gentle guiding of the spirit, while we also try to meet previously established goals? Where is the delicate balance point between structure and inflexibility, between openness and disorder?

Scheduling and Timing Events

The most obvious manifestation of frustration between people with different judging-perceiving preferences comes with scheduling and structuring events. People who prefer judging usually like meetings and events that begin and end on time. They usually like some predictability in the sequence of activities at an event; they like to have a rough idea of what is going to happen. People who prefer perceiving are motivated most of all to stay open to the experience, even if it means being late and even if they have no idea what will happen next.

In congregations we can work hard to encourage the strong judging types to stop making judgmental statements about lateness. Lateness is not a personal affront. It is usually not an aggressive action planned with the intent to hurt people. It is a reflection of someone's absorption in a prior experience.

My own congregation has a perceiving flavor to it. At least half the worshippers arrive each Sunday after the service has started. Most classes, fellowship events, and meetings start late. When I'm in charge of an event, I usually plan on starting five to ten minutes late, no matter who has arrived. That seems to me to reflect a certain level of flexibility, not starting right on the minute, but also not waiting until everyone has arrived. Usually people continue to trail in well after the ten-minute mark.

Our worship service, however, usually starts right on time. Many Sundays only a quarter or a third of the congregation is in their seats when the service starts. If people are late, that is their business. We try to keep critical comments to a minimum.

In meetings, fellowship activities, and other congregational events, we can work to provide a certain amount of structure, while allowing some openness as well. Often it's helpful to articulate our intent to allow both. "Our plan for this newcomer's coffee is to begin by asking three long-time members to share with us what the church means to them. After that, we want you to be free to explore what's interesting to you. There are booths with information about the congregation. You would also be welcome to talk with the people who speak."

In effect, when we describe the agenda for an event, we want to say, "Here are the elements of structure we have provided. Here are the opportunities for flexibility and exploration. We want to provide you with both."

In the Classroom

The same principle applies to the classroom. Participants will find it helpful to know the structure the teacher is expecting to follow, and they will also enjoy knowing where and when they can follow their own curiosity.

It is helpful to open a class session with the same kind of speech mentioned above, a speech that describes the structure of the class session as well as the opportunities for spontaneous exploration. "Today we'll watch a video clip early in the class session. Then we'll discuss the clip in small groups. Before we start the video, I want to give you a few minutes to talk about any specific ideas you'd like to pursue today. And when you're in your small groups, I want you to feel free to bring up any questions you have."

Gordon Lawrence points out that people who prefer perceiving usually enjoy solving problems in their own way. They enjoy studying in order to discover something new to them, and they like to follow their own curiosity spontaneously. This is another argument for using a good amount of discussion in classes. It is also a strong argument for adult classes that genuinely explore complex and difficult issues. Often we who teach in religious settings believe that we have to offer answers to every question. The perceiving preference reminds us that open-ended discussion can be a significant learning experience.

To encourage this aspect of human personality, we can ask questions of the class such as:

- As we address this topic, what are you curious about? What would you like to do to address that curiosity?

- What do you see in this discussion that is new to you?

- What would you like to pursue further as you think about this topic?

Lawrence also describes the educational priorities of people who prefer judging. He says they generally draw energy from the steady, orderly progress of study. They want to know what is expected of them. They usually enjoy clear structure, and they want some kind of closure.

We can address these judging needs in class sessions by paying particular attention to the way we begin and end each class. Beginning by laying out what's ahead is very helpful to people who prefer judging. We can also provide reassurance by ending each class, particularly classes in which there was a lot of discussion, with five minutes of summary. The teacher can provide the summary, or we can continue the discussion by asking class participants to reflect verbally or in a journal on what they thought were the most significant aspects of the class that day. We can also provide a time for silent reflection on what was discussed.

We can also close the class with some kind of small ceremony, such as standing and singing the doxology or standing and holding hands to pray. For a judging type, the very worst kind of class ending is to break off an interesting discussion—or even a boring discussion—with the words, "Goodness! We're out of time. We'll continue next week. See you then." We can serve people who prefer judging by watching the time and allowing five to ten minutes at the end to provide some kind of closure to our class sessions.

Generation X

Each of the generations in our congregations and in our society has characteristics that need to be considered in planning congregational events. It seems clear to me that each of the generations in our society has a different pattern of behavior and a different set of priorities. We can use the language of type to describe some of these differences among the generations.

I don't know of any research that indicates that different generations have a different distribution of types. Even if the types are distributed equally in all generations, it still seems that the generations have particular patterns and values that can be described using the language of type.

The generation born between 1910 and 1930, sometimes called the World War II Generation or the GI Generation, was raised in a time when the values of hard work and perseverance were greatly needed. Duty was an important value. This generation seems to have an STJ flavor because of the events that shaped it.

I don't have a lot of objectivity about the Baby Boom Generation (those born between 1946 and 1964) because I'm right in the middle of it. I suspect that our generation has a stronger intuitive emphasis than the World War II Generation. We like possibilities. We rely heavily on inspiration rather than duty. I suspect that we are still very much a J generation.

The members of the generation born between 1930 and 1946, often called the Silent Generation, seem to take on the attributes of either the generation before (the World War II Generation) or the generation after (the Baby Boom Generation), so their characteristics would be shaped by the generations on either side.

Generation X, those born between 1964 and approximately 1978, pose a significant challenge. We want to welcome that generation to our congregations, but most have very few members of that generation who attend. One striking characteristic of this generation arises out of the judging-perceiving preference.

I believe that Generation X has a pervasive ethos that favors perceiving. They are a generation raised on options, more options than most of us who are slightly older can even imagine. MTV and the Internet illustrate the plethora of possibilities that have shaped this generation. The new and different have been promoted to this generation in millions of ads. Exploration, staying open to new experiences, being stimulated by things that are new and different—all these are characteristics of Generation X, and they are also characteristics of the perceiving preference.

If it is true that most congregations have a judging flavor, then it is no wonder that Generation X is underrepresented in our congregations. We need to think carefully about how we can bring spontaneity and openness back into our congregations without sacrificing that which is important to us.

In interviews for articles I have written about the generations in churches, I have found that those having good attendance by people in their 20s and early 30s share certain characteristics. Many of these characteristics point to a tolerance for the perceiving preference.

Churches with a significant number of Generation X members

almost always use some contemporary music, but not necessarily exclusively. The worship services usually have some informal aspects, such as congregational prayer or open sharing of prayer requests before prayer. There is more flexibility in style in many areas, punctuality is often not a strong value, and extremely informal dress is usually completely accepted. One Presbyterian church with a high percentage of Generation X attenders is known in its presbytery as "the barefoot church" because one 20-something fellow occasionally comes to church barefoot.

The preference for contemporary music may not be connected to a type preference, but every other characteristic listed above relates to a perceiving preference. Embracing this casual, flexible approach will be quite a challenge for many congregations.

Generation X is probably also more oriented to feeling than to thinking. The interconnectedness of all creation and all people is usually important to this generation; it is the first generation to be raised with the theory of relativity rather than Newtonian physics.

It is not too hard to imagine a congregation that embraces the value of feeling in order to welcome people in their 20s and 30s. Many congregations, maybe most congregations, already have an inclination toward feeling. It is probably much more of a stretch to grow in developing the kind of flexibility and openness that this generation needs—the kind of spontaneity that we attribute to the perceiving preference.

All the Preferences

It sometimes seems overwhelming to consider all eight preferences every time we plan an event, teach a class, or preach a sermon. The purpose of this chapter was not to overwhelm anyone. Instead, it was to remind us to be aware, over time, of meeting the needs of all eight preferences.

It can be helpful to start with our own type and reflect on the way our teaching or preaching style reflects our type, or the way the events we plan reflect our type. Then we can begin to consider aspects of other type preferences that we want to be sure are not neglected.

CHAPTER 7

Type and Church Leadership

"I wrote a letter to the pastor last night," Celine told her friend Emily.

"What did it say?" Emily asked.

"I told him I wanted to resign from the board," Celine said with a mischievous glint in her eye.

"What?" Emily shrieked.

"Don't worry too much. . . . I didn't mail the letter." Celine's amused expression became serious. "But after the meeting yesterday, I felt like mailing it. Kyle is driving me crazy. I don't think I can work with him one more minute. You work more closely with him than I do. How can you stand it?"

Celine, INTP, and Emily, ISFP, both serve on their church's governing board. The congregation is in the midst of a huge building campaign, and Kyle, ESTJ, chairs the task force that is raising the money for the new construction. Celine and Emily are members of the task force. Emily, a professional desktop publisher, has worked closely with Kyle designing all the publications for the campaign.

Emily answered Celine's question. "He can be irritating, to be sure, but so can anyone. I'm enjoying working with him because this is the first project where I've felt I can really make a contribution to the church. Finally I have a place to serve using my skills. Kyle has been affirming to me. What is it that bugs you so much about him?"

Celine answered, "He doesn't take the time to analyze anything or consider the possible consequences of his actions. He believes there's only one right way to do things. As a committee, we never brainstorm possible solutions to problems. He wants us to implement his way without discussion. We never discuss possible drawbacks to the one way he wants to do it. I believe there's always more than one way to do things, and I believe it's important to talk about possible outcomes of any plan we undertake. I've tried and tried to suggest that we discuss things, but he is never willing."

Emily answered slowly, "I can see why you're frustrated."

Celine continued. "Asking questions is the foundation for good decisionmaking. Kyle doesn't think deeply; he just starts talking. He only wants to discuss answers, not questions. I still don't see how you can work with him."

"He appreciates my skills, and I like to be appreciated. He just doesn't appreciate your asking questions. I can see that," Emily answered. "But I have a different concern about the fund-raising process. His style is so straightforward, almost brash, that I'm afraid he's offending people in the congregation."

"That's exactly what I mean," Celine responded. "He isn't willing to take the time to consider the possible implications of his actions. The effect they have on people is one of the areas he's not willing to consider."

Using All Four Functions in Decisionmaking

As Kyle leads the task force, he is working out of his dominant and auxiliary functions. He gathers data through sensing (focusing on the facts), and he makes decisions through thinking (responding logically to those facts). His approach is straightforward and his thinking processes are not hidden from the task force, but he is missing some of the possible long-term implications of his actions and he is not giving adequate consideration to the effects of his actions on people. Addressing the possible long-term implications of our actions comes out of our intuitive function, and taking into account the effect of our actions on people draws on our feeling function. Kyle needs help to be reminded to use those functions, too.

As an ISFP, Emily's dominant function is feeling, so she is particularly aware of the effects of decisions on other people. She herself is feeling affirmed and needed by Kyle, so she is able to cope with her low-level frustration at his occasional lack of consideration for others.

Kyle (ESTJ) and Celine (INTP) both have the same dominant function—thinking. It would be easy to believe that they would get along well because of that fact. However, Kyle's dominant extraverted thinking and Celine's dominant introverted thinking are actually very different, particularly because their auxiliary functions (sensing and intuition) are opposite.

I have observed that often the people who are hardest for me to get along with are those with every letter opposite of mine or those who have the same dominant function that I have, but who use it in the opposite attitude (introversion or extraversion), like Kyle and Celine. It will take an extra effort for these two to appreciate each other and to rely on each other's strengths. The group decisionmaking process will be healthier if they can defer to each other to some extent.

Some of this natural difference of viewpoint can be smoothed over by consciously choosing to use each of the four functions in group decisionmaking. Each of the four functions has an important role to play as a group considers what to do in any situation.

Any committee, task force, or board can decide ahead of time to embrace a four-step process of decisionmaking based on the four functions. Or a meeting chairperson can try to keep in mind these four aspects of decisionmaking. Any group member could keep these four steps in mind and ask questions at the appropriate time.

Sensing

When we use sensing, we are focusing on the facts. At the beginning of any decisionmaking process, it is helpful to start with the journalistic questions: who, what, when, where, and how. All details and facts that pertain to the situation should be considered. Sensing focuses on *what is*.

In the case of raising money for a building project, this is the time for the task force to consider all the issues concerning money. How much will the construction cost? Can the scope of the project be reduced if adequate money is not raised? What is the time frame? What people are available to participate in fund-raising in all kinds of different roles? Can the congregation photocopy machine be used to print materials? Is there a bulk mail permit that can be used? What are the existing financial resources? Many other such questions can be asked.

People who have a preference for intuition may find this process boring. The listed facts seem painfully obvious to them. Intuitives usually want to jump to the second step: considering possibilities. They need to remind themselves that the facts form the foundation for generating possibilities. They also need to remind themselves that the people on the committee, board, or task force who prefer sensing will be very frustrated by jumping rapidly to brainstorming. Sensing details are important to consider because the outcome must be based on adequate information. Sensing details are also important because many of the people involved will be frustrated if these facts are overlooked.

Intuition

When the sensing facts and details have been enumerated, move into the area of intuition. Intuition considers *what could* be. Consider these questions: What do the facts mean? What possibilities do they suggest? Search for meaning, themes, relationships, and connections. Don't leave the realm of intuition before you have brainstormed at least several possible solutions to the problem or several possible plans for the project.

This is the arena that is uncomfortable for Kyle, so he habitually short-circuits brainstorming. Often people who prefer sensing do not enjoy taking time to discuss the meaning of the facts and the possibilities suggested by the facts. They need to remind themselves that an excellent plan can't be implemented if it has never been dreamed of.

Thinking

When we move to the area of thinking, we objectively evaluate the possible plans and solutions. We use logic to discuss the pros and cons of all the ideas that have been generated when brainstorming. We evaluate the ways that the possible plans and solutions meet the objective needs outlined using sensing. We consider the possible outcomes of the various options we have discussed.

Kyle does a good job of understanding and communicating the possible outcomes of the one plan he wants to implement, but because the brainstorming process was cut short, the thinking process is also truncated. The ability to use thinking analysis effectively depends on having both information and possibilities to analyze.

Feeling

After using logic to analyze the possible plans and solutions, continue to
analyze using your values. What impact would these plans or solutions
have on our priorities as a group and as individuals? What is important
to me? What is important to us? How might each of us react to our possible plans? How might others in the congregation react? How might each
of our plans or solutions affect the congregation or the wider community?
    Certainly it is not possible to please all of the people all of the time.
Considering feeling values in part addresses the issue of how people will
react and whether they will be pleased or not. But considering feeling
values addresses deeper issues, too, about our values and priorities as a
community. Making a decision based entirely on logic and efficiency,
without considering the impact on people, is very unwise, particularly in
a faith community.[1]

Using Type Categories without Type Vocabulary

During the decisionmaking process in a committee or task force, it is
possible to bring some of these type-related considerations into the discussion without ever mentioning type. A group leader or a participant
can raise various kinds of questions.
    If we believe that the sensing process of gathering information is
being short-circuited, we can say:

- I'm not sure we've gathered enough information yet. Could we
  slow down for a minute and spend a little more time considering. . .
- I'm not ready to begin brainstorming solutions yet. I think we
  need more information, particularly about . . .
- I've got a question we could discuss before we move into brainstorming options. Suppose someone from outside our congregation came to our meeting. What questions would they ask about
  our resources as we begin this project?

If we feel that intuition has been neglected, we can say:

- I'm not sure we've looked at all the data thoroughly. We haven't
  discussed all the possible interpretations of these facts.

- I'm not clear yet on what these facts mean. Could we discuss that before we move into analysis?
- I'm not comfortable with immediately adopting one plan. Could we take some time to brainstorm other possible options? There might be another plan that's better and we won't discover it unless we take some time to explore.

If we believe that the decision is not being evaluated analytically using thinking, we can say:

- Before we move on, could we discuss the pros and cons of these options a little longer?
- I'm not sure we've covered all the possible outcomes or consequences. Before we decide, can we spend more time considering what might happen if we implement this plan?

If we are concerned that people values have been neglected in the discussion, we might say:

- Before we make a decision, could we please talk about our values as a congregation and how this decision might build on our values?
- Could we talk for a little while about the ways this decision is important to each of us and the ways it would be important to others in the congregation?
- Can we please discuss the ways this decision might affect people in the congregation?

It is very helpful for a group to decide together that each of the four functions—sensing, intuition, thinking, and feeling—should be represented in the decisionmaking process. Then group members can remind each other not to neglect any of these considerations. But even without knowledge about type on the part of everyone in the group, the questions listed above can be used by the chairperson of the meeting or by an individual participant.

Each of us who leads committees, task forces, or boards needs to consider the ways we short-circuit effective decisionmaking by neglecting the considerations that don't come easily to us. We can keep handy a stock of questions that address our weak areas and allow the group to explore the issue from a different angle.

Typing a Congregation

Two weeks have passed since Celine talked with Emily about her frustrations with the building campaign. The task force has met one more time, and Celine called Emily the day after the meeting.

"I'm clearer on what's making me frustrated," Celine told Emily over the phone.

"What is it?" Emily answered.

"There's a discrepancy between Kyle's style of leading this campaign and our congregation's normal way of functioning. We're a laid-back, informal congregation and Kyle is charging into this campaign like an army general. He has specific deadlines for people to make their pledges. In fact, his timeline for the whole campaign seems rigid. I think people aren't going to respond very well because they're going to feel railroaded."

"I can see what you're talking about," Emily answered. "I've been concerned all along that Kyle seems pushy and that people might feel hurt or angry by the way he communicates. Our congregation values outreach to the poor and needy, and it seems to value compassion and caring, but Kyle is presenting this building campaign only as a way for us to be more comfortable in our own building."

"That's a slightly different issue," Celine answered, with her characteristic INTP analytical viewpoint. "People's sensitivity to their values is not the same as their desire not to be pushed."

Emily responded, "In our congregation they're related to each other. And Kyle doesn't seem to value either one."

Celine and Emily are talking about typing their congregation, even though they aren't using that vocabulary. Celine has noticed the congregation's laid-back style, a characteristic of the perceiving preference. Emily has noticed the congregation's strong commitment to compassion, a characteristic of the feeling preference. This FP congregation is being challenged by a building campaign led by Kyle with his TJ preferences. It is not surprising that Celine and Emily have concerns about the effectiveness of the campaign.

It can be very helpful to spend some time trying to type a congregation. Understanding the congregation's habitual way of functioning—its "type"—can provide insight in many areas and can make programming and staffing more effective. It would be possible to administer the MBTI to everyone in the congregation and look for patterns. However, the most common type patterns within a congregation may not be the same as the type of the congregation. Interestingly enough, the congregation itself often has a predominant flavor that is slightly different, or even very different, from the majority of its members. A system is more than the sum of its parts.

In *The Character of Organizations,* management consultant William Bridges discusses the type or character, as he calls it, of organizations. He believes that an organization's type can be influenced by its founder, its subsequent leaders, its leadership team, or any other influential group within the organization. In the case of businesses, Bridges believes that the employee group contributes to an organization's character, but they do not necessarily determine it.[2] When considering the origins of a church's type, we would take into account past and present pastors, other staff, the congregation's influential lay leaders, and its denomination.

The following characteristics will help you type your congregation.[3] Bridges warns that it usually takes a group of people to figure out an organization's type. Any one person's perceptions may be inaccurate.

Extraversion and Introversion

Extraverted congregations tend to welcome newcomers effectively. They often enjoy holding fellowship events that welcome large numbers of people. They will probably be concerned about outreach to the community, and they will probably be responsive to the demographics and needs in their neighborhoods. They may be concerned about the external appearance of the building, and they would be particularly concerned that the building communicate that the congregation is a welcoming place. The decisionmaking processes and inner workings of the leadership will probably be fairly transparent, and the congregation would understand where decisions come from. Congregational members and leaders will probably collaborate fairly easily on projects.

Introverted congregations tend to be concerned that they are providing a place for people to meet God individually. They may enjoy holding contemplative prayer events. They will probably be more concerned about whether the congregation is ministering to its members than to its neighborhood. They may be concerned about the interior of the building, particularly whether it communicates the primacy of a personal relationship with God. The direction of the introverted congregation is more likely to come from the inner vision of its leaders rather than from felt needs of the congregation and the neighborhood. The decisionmaking process of the leadership may be invisible; it may seem to congregation members that decisions appear mysteriously. Collaboration by members and/or leaders may feel awkward and come only after individual opinions and plans are established.

Sensing and Intuition

Sensing congregations will be concerned with the past and the present. They will enjoy being up-to-date in the practical, concrete matters of running a congregation: the finances, the grounds, and the building. They will probably have operational procedures or policy manuals covering many areas of congregational life. When changes occur they will outline a step-by-step plan. The nuts and bolts of the congregation's life will probably be a concern of the board, and decisions will be made based on the actualities of the situation. The leadership of the congregation will be described as down-to-earth and solid, and it will value practicality and reliability. Faithfulness to the tried-and-true will usually be a characteristic of a sensing congregation.

Intuitive congregations will be energized by considering the future and the overall vision of the congregation. They will want to be on the cutting edge of new opportunities. The board will strive to keep in view an overarching picture of the congregation and its goals and future possibilities. When change occurs, conversations will be dominated by discussion of the vision for where things are going, and the change will usually be faced as a whole, as one transformational leap, rather than step-by-step. The leadership will be described as intuitive and visionary, and it will value acting ingenuously and inventively.

Thinking and Feeling

Feeling congregations will usually be motivated by compassion, and this concern will be reflected in ministries within the congregation and outreach beyond the congregation. They will be concerned about keeping as many people as possible in the congregation happy. Affect and atmosphere will be important considerations, more important than efficient systems. Relationships will be valued as highly as tasks. An important goal of serving in the congregation will be that members are able to exercise their individual talents fully. Personnel issues will revolve around individual circumstances and considerations. "Communication" will usually mean staying in touch with congregation members. Leaders will be motivated to consider the humane and sensitive thing to do in difficult situations.

Thinking congregations will be motivated by reason and truth. This may be reflected in a commitment to adult education. Thinking congregations will often be able to make tough decisions and confront people with unpleasant truths. Clarity and accuracy will be important considerations. The congregation will probably value efficient systems, and tasks will be more important than relationships. When people serve, the highest consideration will be that they fulfill their roles effectively. Personnel issues will center around general principles and standards. "Communication" will probably mean providing information. Leaders will be motivated to consider the logical and rational thing to do in difficult situations.

Judging and Perceiving

The judging congregation will be characterized by structures, schedules, and plans, with a commitment to being organized and methodical. Meetings will usually be planned well in advance, with agendas that are sent out ahead of time. Events will also be planned well in advance, they will start on time, and the building will be clean and neat. Details of policies and procedures will probably be spelled out. Systematic and careful planning will be a priority. Decisionmaking will be quick and efficient. If the congregation and its leaders have a fault, it is that they jump into decisions too quickly.

Perceiving congregations will be characterized by openness and
spontaneity, with a commitment to being flexible and adaptive. Meetings may have an impromptu flavor, with an agenda that emerges as the
meeting progresses. Some level of disorder is tolerated in the building,
and meetings and events often start and end late. Policies will be established only seldom; the absence of policies will be seen as enabling
people to work in their own best style. Rather than planning ahead,
congregation leaders often make it up as they go along. Leaders will
probably consider issues from every angle. If the congregation and its
leaders have a fault, it is that they keep options open for too long.

Responding to Your Congregation's Type

After you figure out your congregation's type, you can begin to discuss
how to respond. William Bridges believes that there are only four ways
to deal wisely with the strengths and weaknesses of any organization:

- Avoid its weaknesses. The congregation can choose to avoid
  projects and plans that require strengths the congregation doesn't
  have.
- Compensate for its weaknesses. The congregation can find external resources to make up for its weak areas. This could include
  linking up with a parachurch or ecumenical ministry, or part-
  nering with a neighboring congregation.
- Develop new strengths. Congregational leaders can consciously
  choose to embrace change in the direction of growth in weak
  areas. They may choose to encourage lay leaders or hire staff
  who have strengths that are opposite from those of the congregation in one or more areas.
- Capitalize on its existing strengths. A congregation can decide to
  go forward in directions that draw on its strengths.[4]

Considering your congregation's type and looking at Bridges' four
options for response can be very helpful, because it brings into con-
sciousness significant patterns that are usually not discussed or acknowl-
edged.

Comparing Pastors, Congregations, and Leadership Boards

Comparing and contrasting the pastor's type with the congregation can be a fascinating endeavor. It may explain some long-standing conflicts and irritations. In the same way we can type a congregation, we can type a leadership board, then compare the board's type with those of the congregation and the pastor. Again, this may explain patterns of communication and conflict fairly readily, and it may become clear how to compensate for the dominant type pattern in order to draw on the type preferences that aren't as common in the congregation.

One congregation's leaders observed that the community around the congregation seemed to be oriented to sensing, so they tried to bring more sensing components into their worship in order to attract the community. Comparing the congregation's type to that of the type of the neighborhood can make for a fruitful discussion. This is not an exact science, and some congregation leaders may find this kind of discussion too vague and imprecise. It may be easier for some people to accept statements like, "Our building isn't welcoming to the community," rather than "Our congregation must be introverted because we don't put any emphasis on making our building welcoming from the outside." The goal of these discussions is to promote more effective ministry. Figuring out a congregation's type or that of the surrounding community is not an end in itself.

Considering the relationship between the type of the pastor and of the congregation can be very helpful. In any type pairing, whether it is a pastor and congregation or a husband and wife, there are potential strengths and problems. Some of the same dynamics are at work in the pastor-congregation relationship as we find in marriage.

If a husband and wife both have preferences for judging, for example, there will be some advantages. They will probably be able to make decisions easily and their household will probably be orderly. There will also be disadvantages to this pairing. The couple may make decisions too quickly because they have grown tired of collecting data. They may lack flexibility and playfulness. They may work so hard that they don't leave time for fun.

Some of the same patterns will probably be true of a congregation and pastor who both prefer judging. There will be advantages because there will be a minimum of conflict in that area, but they may appear inflexible and rigid to outsiders. The whole congregational system may not be open to new information or possible changes. Possibilities for growth and development may be stunted.

In a marriage, if one partner prefers judging and the other prefers perceiving, there will be more balance and mutual growth. The J will probably make plans, and the P will add adventure and spontaneity. The J will provide the stimulus to get chores done, and the P will provide the stimulus to play and enjoy life. The combination can be very healthy for both.

However, this J-P couple will probably have conflicts about timing and decisionmaking. The P may consider the J to be too serious and may feel boxed in by the J's need for structure. The J may consider the P to be irresponsible and may feel discomfort over the P's unwillingness to make plans or schedule things. Yet the couple has the potential to make excellent decisions because the P will make sure enough data are gathered and the J will make sure the decision is made in a timely manner.

In the same way, when the congregation-pastor pairing involves both judging and perceiving, there may be hurt and misunderstanding, but there is great potential for growth and excellence.

Although Kyle, the building-campaign committee chair, is not a pastor, his situation illustrates the possible benefits of a difference in type between pastors (or leaders) and congregations. Kyle, with his TJ preferences, may end up being a highly effective building campaign organizer for an FP congregation because he may bring strengths to the building campaign that would otherwise be lacking. That's the irony of discussing type in congregations. Often the most effective leader or pastor is the one who has preferences different from those of the congregation. But in order to be effective, the pastor or leader has to make concessions to prevailing type climate within the congregation.

If Kyle can listen to the members of his task force and gain some gentle flexibility as he plans his timeline, he might supply just the right amount of order and closure that the congregation needs in order to raise a large sum of money.

I am convinced it is no accident that a majority of people in congregations have a preference for sensing, while a majority of clergy prefer intuition. Certainly demographics alone contribute to this phenomenon, but interpersonal dynamics also play a part. Congregations call pastors who seem to be able to bring what the congregation needs. The intuitive concern for big-picture vision often provides just the right challenge for a congregation absorbed in the sensing, nuts-and-bolts details of congregational life. But the intuitive pastor, in order to minister effectively, needs continually to strive to be sensitive to the congregation's sensing needs. Intuitive insight, supported with just enough sensing detail, can be very powerful.

After comparing the congregation's type with the pastor's, consider each of the other pairings—congregation and board, board and pastor, and congregation and neighborhood—and look for the strengths and potential problems of the pairings.

When there is similarity of type there will probably be less conflict and less growth. The key question to address is how much you want to compensate for the missing type preferences and how much you want to go with the strengths of the types present and avoid the commensurate weaknesses.

When there are differences of type, there will probably be more conflict and more growth. The key issue will be creating a way to appreciate the differences and learning to rely on each other's strengths. A lot of conversation will be necessary, but the end product may be excellent indeed.

Conflict

Some conflict arises because we don't understand differences between ourselves and others. Kyle's ESTJ matter-of-fact, decisive style may seem arrogant and insensitive to someone with a feeling preference, particularly someone with FP preferences. It is one thing to say or think, "Kyle's bulldozer style irritates me because I really want to be sure that everyone is heard before we move ahead." We move to another level of misunderstanding when we believe that Kyle is being malicious or deliberately insensitive. This can lead to painful and damaging conflict.

Kyle tends to move quickly to the planning and implementing stage in a project. That is simply his personality style. There is usually nothing malicious about it. He is not trying to be deliberately hurtful. Type can help us work with others in our congregation by giving us vocabulary and concepts to describe these differences in style. Once we understand them, we can be more gentle and also more assertive in asking that other styles be affirmed and included. This understanding can help us avoid falling into the trap of attributing evil to people when their styles differ from ours, and it can prevent conflict from escalating to damaging levels.

As much as understanding type can help diffuse conflict, it certainly does not remove the deep-seated differences among people. We may be able to see very clearly the type differences that make conflict likely, but we still have to be willing to engage in long conversations and negotiations in order to avoid that conflict or in order to resolve conflict that has already started. It is hard work to listen to someone with a different perspective than our own, particularly when our values and way of doing things are at stake.

Type and Change

Congregations frequently experience change. Some changes are obvious and visible. A pastor leaves and the search for a new pastor begins. A longtime congregational leader dies. The congregation starts construction of a new building or decides to add onto its existing building.

Some of the changes we face in congregations are more subtle. Perhaps a new freeway extension wipes out part of the neighborhood church and it takes months for the congregation to realize its ministry has been affected. Or maybe a neighborhood slowly changes in its ethnic composition or its median age, and the congregation finds itself an island in the midst of an environment very different from itself. Possibly more young people have joined a congregation and the worship has gradually become more informal.

Sometimes we are the agents of change. If we are serving on the board that makes the decision about new construction, the change makes sense to us because we were involved in the process of gathering and processing information. The change may feel to us like an exciting opportunity. To someone who was not involved in the decision, the change may feel sudden, disorienting, and confusing.

All change involves coping with loss. Nancy Barger and Linda Kirby, consultants who teach and write about type, describe the implications of type in a changing environment in *Type and Change*. Their research indicates that the thinking-feeling preference is the most significant when considering the impact of loss. Thinking and feeling types will each have strengths and potential problem areas when facing loss.

They write that people with a preference for thinking "usually have the ability to put their emotions aside to focus on tasks or decisions."[5] They are often able to step back and apply impersonal logic. This can be a real asset, particularly in a crisis. They often have the ability to separate and move on.

The danger is that thinking types "may detach from their own emotions, telling themselves, 'It's not logical to feel angry just because I have a different view outside my window.'"[6] They can feel powerless to deal with strong emotions, particularly negative ones, and they may have difficulty assessing their own emotions accurately. If they don't process their emotions, they may later experience repercussions such as depression or anger. In addition, Barger and Kirby write, they may "become uncomfortable and impatient with others' emotions."[7]

In contrast, people with feeling preferences "are attuned to their own emotional states and also to those of others."[8] They are able to acknowledge that complex emotions are natural in times of loss. This ability usually makes them good listeners, so the people around them feel accepted and cared for. This process of engaging with others in time of loss often enables them to feel connected themselves, which is important in the midst of change.

But the commensurate disadvantage is that they can become paralyzed by their own emotions as well as by the powerful emotions of others that they are also able to feel. They can find it very difficult to move on, to problem-solve, and to decide which tasks to undertake next. Sometimes they have a hard time seeing when it is time to leave the negative emotions behind and move on.

Feeling types may believe that thinking types are moving too fast, ignoring the very real emotions in the situation. Thinking types may believe that feeling types are moving too slowly, getting enmeshed in everyone's pain rather than addressing the issues that need to be faced. Both viewpoints have elements of truth, and gentle exhortation based on these principles would be appropriate in the midst of change.

In the midst of congregational change, it will be helpful to consider each of the type preferences and make sure information and opportunities are provided for all the various needs.[9]

Extraverts need a lot of information. In order to give enough information to extraverts, it may feel to introverts that they are overcommunicating. Extraverts will feel left out if they are not given lots of information so they can understand what is going on. They will also probably need opportunities to discuss the changes. Changes in their community and relationships will probably be significant to them.

Introverts will probably need time to reflect before joining in. They usually appreciate written information. Changes in their personal space will probably be significant to them.

Sensing types need specific information, with concrete and practical examples. They will also probably benefit from discussing how change will affect the way things are currently done.

Intuitives need to be informed of the big picture. They will probably appreciate an opportunity to discuss the long-term implications of the change. They will feel connected to the change if they are able to help design some aspects of the situation.

Thinking types need opportunities to ask questions. They will look for fairness and justice as the change is implemented. They will probably enjoy participating by having the chance to help develop new systems.

Feeling types will want to consider the way the changes will affect them and other people. They will probably feel a part of the change if they can discuss the ways the situation will influence their values and priorities.

People with judging preferences will probably appreciate knowing the schedule for the change. They usually need a sense of closure, so benchmarks in the process will be helpful.

People with perceiving preferences usually need assurance that there will be possibilities for mid-course corrections of schedules and plans. They will appreciate having opportunities to use their spontaneity and flexibility.

Major change is so stressful that we tend to go on autopilot, working out of our strongest preferences. In the midst of congregational change, perhaps more than at any other time, we need to remind ourselves of the variety of human needs and the diversity of human personality, so that we can try to meet at least some of the needs of all the people involved.

Change and the Congregational System

In *The Character of Organizations* William Bridges explores the impact of change on organizations. Many of his observations are relevant to congregations.

Extraversion and Introversion

In times of congregational change that comes from an outside force, an extraverted congregation is more likely to respond with some degree of comfort, because extraverted organizations "carry on a natural dialogue with their environment, picking up clues, testing out responses, and seeking external evaluations of what they are doing."[10] This interaction with the outer world prepares extraverted congregations for changes that come from outside and enables them to reorient themselves.

Introverted congregations will probably be slower to respond to such outside forces and may resist responding. They are more reluctant to let in external signals, and they process information from outside more slowly. When they do acknowledge the inevitability of a particular change, they are likely to express impatience, "not just because (like any organization) their plans have been disrupted, but because the external world is always experienced by the introverted organization as to some extent intrusive and as a distraction from the real business that the organization is engaged in."[11]

Some changes originate within the congregation, and introverted congregations will be more likely to adapt to those changes fairly easily. These changes include new needs of members, or transitions because of growth or loss of membership. Extraverted congregations, on the other hand, can be almost immobilized by developmental passages because they are much less likely to have seen the change coming.

Sensing and Intuition

Bridges uses a helpful analogy to see the different responses to change by sensing and intuitive organizations. The present focus of a sensing organization is like a light that clearly illuminates the path it is on, but the light is focused only one step ahead. The future focus of an intuitive congregation will also provide a light to illuminate the path, but it will be focused way ahead. Therefore, a sensing congregation will respond better to present realities, but may be totally out of touch with what lies ahead. The intuitive congregation will be more likely to see future problems and issues, but will also be more likely to be tripped up by immediate problems.

Sensing congregations will prefer to walk through change in a step-by-step fashion. They will talk about "the wisdom of incremental change —about how it allows you to keep what is good and improve the rest, how it allows you to make mid-course corrections."[12] In intuitive congregations "you will hear how piecemeal changes lead to uneven results, how you need an overall design to integrate the whole project. . . . The intuitive organization has more faith in the big, once-and-for-all change in which the whole system is transformed."[13] At the same time the intuitive organization, writes Bridges, is "vulnerable to infatuation with its own imaginings."[14]

Thinking and Feeling

In the midst of change, the thinking congregation has a natural advantage because it will embrace analysis and planning as a way of coping with the demands of the new situation. The feeling congregation will be unenthusiastic about such a cut-and-dried response because it will be more focused on caring for the people impacted by the change. The strength of a feeling congregation in the midst of change is its automatic consideration of the human issues.

Responding to people's needs in the midst of all the transitions that occur around a change may be difficult for a thinking congregation because members are likely to believe that "if a change is logical, everyone will accept it and adjust to it."[15] A feeling congregation is more likely to care for the personal needs of its members.

Feeling congregations will be more likely to embrace change if the impetus has to do with the congregations' values. Thinking congregations are more likely to embrace change if the reasons are logical. Both types of congregations are likely to talk about the right thing to do in the midst of change, but the thinking congregation will define "the right thing to do" as the rational or effective thing, while the feeling congregation will mean the humane or wise thing.

Judging and Perceiving

Judging congregations are likely to view change as an intrusive disruption in the midst of the otherwise natural state of peaceful stability. Perceiving congregations are more likely to view change as normal and healthy. Perceiving congregations, however, will find change difficult when the change is in the direction of more structure. For example, when a new congregation reaches the size at which more support structure is needed, the very characteristic that made the congregation flexible, responsive to new people, and adventurous in the start-up phase, will now push the congregation to resist the structure necessary for further growth.

Because change is inevitable, because change always involves some sort of loss, and because people respond so differently to change and loss, these are significant issues to discuss in congregations. Understanding type can help us communicate effectively so that individuals in our congregations can have resources to cope with loss and change. Understanding our congregation's type and the implications of type for organizational change can help us facilitate smoother transitions, and we may also avoid being blindsided by unexpected forces in the midst of change.

CHAPTER 8

Type and Pastoral Care

Salvadore, ISTP, has lost his job and is suffering from major health problems. He has been to see his pastor twice for counseling. What he wants most of all is for someone to listen to him and to reassure him that God loves him in the midst of his life crisis.

Salvadore isn't sure of his pastor's type, but he figures the pastor is probably an extravert because he seems to do so much talking. Even though Salvadore has a preference for thinking, he gets tired of the pattern of problem solving that thinking types fall into so easily. Salvadore can see his pastor trying to solve the issues raised by his situation rather than actively listening to what Salvadore has to say. Salvadore had been hoping that the pastor would be able to listen sympathetically, the way his mother had when he was a child. He remembered so vividly the conversations with his mother at the kitchen table. By sitting quietly and listening to his whole story, she conveyed to Salvadore her confidence that Salvadore had the resources to cope with the difficult situation. He had never found another listener like his mother. He had been hoping to find it in his pastor.

Considering Our Own Type in Pastoral Counseling

Engaging in the kind of careful listening required when people are in pain or in crisis, we need to be aware of the natural tendencies of our own type, some of which may not always be helpful. This is an important consideration for pastors, Stephen or BeFriender Ministers, small group leaders, or simply a friend providing a listening ear. We need to consider the same issues described in chapter 5 in the context of spiritual direction. Extraverts need to watch their tendency to talk too much; introverted intuitives need to be quiet about many of their insights; thinkers need to limit their verbal analyzing; and so on.

The ministry of presence required when people are in great need may come easiest to listeners with a perceiving preference. Unlike spiritual direction in which the director may want to make assignments and provide structure for the directee, listening to people in crisis or pain involves bringing God's presence into a situation without a lot of structure or directives. Therefore, pastoral caregivers with a preference for judging need to guard against their need for closure or problem solving.

In spiritual direction, directors can take the time to administer a type inventory as they get to know the directee. In pastoral-care listening, particularly if the care recipient is in crisis, there simply isn't time and it isn't appropriate to test for type. Sometimes the caregiver knows the person fairly well and has a fair idea of the type preferences. Other times, the caregiver can watch the response to specific questions to get some idea of the care recipient's type.

In *Voices of Loss* Charles W. Ginn, a psychologist who conducts seminars on the grieving process, notes that when we are in pain or crisis we tend to rely more than usual on our dominant function.[1] He suggests that when we want to provide a listening ear to someone in need, it is most helpful to ask questions related to the person's dominant function.

Dominant intuitives, since they are oriented to future hope, will respond best to questions like: What do you hope for in this situation? What would enable you to experience more hope? In what ways can you see this situation resolving itself in the future? What kind of support will you need in the future? What do you think will be helpful in the weeks ahead? What steps do you want to take now to meet some of these future needs?

Because intuitives are oriented to the future, they often feel overwhelmed when they can't generate hope. This is common when under stress. The caregiver can help by asking questions that enable the intuitive to rediscover hope, even if it is centered around some very small aspect of the situation.

When in pain, dominant sensors will not enjoy talking about the future. They are oriented to the present, so helpful questions should focus on the present. What are you feeling now? What would be helpful to you right now? What facts are most important to note about today's situation? How do you want to respond to this situation today? What concerns are most pressing right now?

Dominant thinkers will probably have a high need to analyze the situation. They will probably feel comfortable exploring its causes. It may be helpful to ask what questions they are mulling over as they consider this difficult situation. Because thinkers need to figure things out, they can be paralyzed when in pain because they believe they should have been able to foresee this situation or prevent it from happening. It is important that they be able to voice their feelings of powerlessness.

Because the thinking function can look cold and unfeeling, it is not unusual for a dominant thinking type to appear completely insensitive to the feelings of others when in pain. Because many caregivers have feeling preferences, they may be offended by the thinker's apparent cold self-absorption. It is important to recognize that all of us become self-absorbed when in pain. Self-absorption simply looks different depending on type.

Dominant feelers, when in crisis or pain, will be highly attuned to the people around them. They will be very sensitive to perceived slights or possible disharmony. They will need to discuss questions around relationships. In what ways are you concerned about the others in this situation? What are your concerns about your relationships with them? How do you hope to be of support to them? What kind of support do you need from them? What would it take for you to ask for that support? What are the obstacles to asking?

If we don't know the care recipient's dominant function, we can try questions from each of the four areas, watching to see which kinds of questions seem to enable the person to talk about what's important to him or her. Practical suggestions that we make to people in crisis or in pain need to address their dominant function. To the feelers, we might give encouragement to connect with loved ones. To the thinkers, we may suggest that they spend some time thinking about the questions they raised with us. To the intuitives, we could give encouragement to hold onto the small fragments of hope they have identified. To the sensors, we can suggest that they work on addressing some of the present needs they have identified.

Pastoral care in pain or crisis is primarily a ministry of presence, helping a person to know God is with them in their pain. Occasionally confrontation becomes necessary, particularly when we have reason to think a person is evading a difficult issue. First of all, we have to determine whether the other person is indeed evading an important question or whether a difference in communication style has led us to a false conclusion. Charles Ginn suggests that we say something like, "It might be a result of our different approaches, but when I heard you say ___ , I didn't pick up any of the concern I would have expected."[2] Understanding type differences can give us the humility to ask for information in the midst of confronting some aspect of the situation, so that we don't make too many inaccurate assumptions.

When a person is in crisis or pain, it's not the time to make suggestions about growing in their less-preferred areas. That will come later, in the healing stages, when the person is ready to leave some of the pain behind and move on. That would be an ideal time to suggest a few new things based on a less-preferred function, such as a new pattern of prayer or a new avenue of service. In the midst of the intense pain, however, we can help people rely on their dominant function—the one they have developed most fully and use most competently and comfortably.

Premarriage Counseling

Some pastors use type in premarriage counseling. Several pastors who use type have told me that the most common question asked by engaged couples is, "Should people of our two types marry each other? What are the chances that our marriage will last?" It is important to reassure engaged couples that there are happily married couples of every possible type combination. Couples with every letter the same can be happy together, as can couples with every letter different, or any other possible combination.

Using type in premarriage counseling can be valuable because it can provide a structure for engaged couples to explore differences. Usually type provides a vocabulary for couples to express some of the differences they had already noticed. One pastor told me that discussing type helps engaged couples break through—however briefly—the fog of infatuation that typically surrounds them.

It is not realistic to believe that deep-seated differences will emerge in premarital counseling by using type. Because of this common "fog of infatuation," the best we can expect is to bring to light some of the issues that may cause problems later, with the hope that the couple might remember some of the discussion when problems arise.

Using type in premarital counseling requires a fair amount of time, probably a minimum of three sessions. The basics of type must be explained, and then there needs to be time to explore the implications of the differences and similarities.

Marriage Counseling

Again, type can be helpful because it provides a vocabulary to describe differences. In addition, some of the problems in a marriage may arise from type similarities.

Margaret Hartzler and Gary Hartzler, consultants and writers on many type issues, have written *Using Type with Couples*. In it they present the strengths and problems of each type pairing.

For example, the Hartzlers write that when two extraverts are married to each other, the areas of strength will include their enjoyment of being active and doing a lot together. They will probably enjoy having people around, and they will probably talk to each other easily. The problem areas for two extraverts married to each other are that they may be so busy they don't have enough time together. They may have trouble listening to each other and they may compete with each other for airtime.[3]

The Hartzlers have also written lists of the possible strengths and weaknesses of two introverts married to each other, as well as an introvert married to an extravert. Then they go through each of the other possible type-preference pairings in marriage.

Their lists illustrate the important principle that there are good and bad points in any type pairing. For example, my husband and I are different in every type preference except the last. We both have preferences for judging. We have learned over the years to respect and draw on each other's differences. Our common judging preference causes us just as much trouble as the areas that are different. We both like closure, which is nice, but we often have a hard time playing together because we would both rather get our work finished before we play. And there is always more work to be done!

When using type in marriage counseling, it is important to acknowledge that problems and blessings can arise from type preferences that are different, as well as from type preferences that are alike.

Ministry to Families

Type has significant implications in parenting. My husband and I have major differences in parenting style. For example, I (with a preference for thinking) feel strongly that impartial justice based on clearly established guidelines is a way we serve our children and prepare them for life as adults. My husband (with a preference for feeling) would much rather not have to discipline anyone, ever. If he has to administer any kind of discipline, he prefers to consider each case individually.

Type can be helpful to parents in any stage of parenting. With more blended families in our congregations, merging of parenting styles is more of an issue than ever before. Type can be a helpful tool in pastoral care with families, allowing parents to explore their priorities and styles in parenting.

Two communications consultants, Janet Penley and Diane Stephens, have written an excellent resource for using type and parenting, *The M.O.M.S. Handbook.* The acronym M.O.M.S. comes from a nationwide organization called Mothers of Many Styles. The handbook describes the parenting issues raised by our type preferences. The second half of the book describes the mothering style of each of the 16 types. Almost every one of my strengths and weaknesses as a mother is described on the INTJ page,[4] and they didn't even interview me!

The handbook could be used for a parenting class in a congregation. Even though the book focuses on mothering styles, many of the same issues are relevant to fathers. In the same way that pastors need to consider the implications of their own type as they engage in pastoral care or spiritual direction or sermon preparation, parents can benefit from discussing together the ramifications of their type as they raise their children.

A totally different approach is presented in the book *Nurture by Nature* by Paul Tieger and Barbara Barron-Tieger,[5] authors of a previous book on type and career choice. In *Nurture by Nature* they explore personality type in children and offer suggestions for the nurture of children based on the child's type.

I am very wary of labelling children with type categories when they are too young. What is too young? Experts vary in their opinion. Some people in the type community believe that some type preferences are visible virtually from birth. Others believe that children have to be well into their teen years before the type preferences become completely visible.

Nature by Nurture could certainly be used in congregations as a part of evaluating the children's program. Are all the possible type preferences in children being addressed? In addition, pastors could use the book to help parents struggling through problems with their children. It provides a useful framework to explore the differences in children's needs resulting from type differences. If nothing else, the book reminds us to avoid the common pitfall of believing that there is one style of godly parenting. Each unique child needs what is right for him or her.

Confirmation Class

One church uses type as a part of its confirmation process. In that congregation, confirmation takes place at about age 15. Each member of the confirmation class takes the Myers-Briggs Type Indicator, and the group discusses the implications of type, particularly as it relates to spiritual development.

If you want to administer a type instrument to anyone under 18, it is important to get permission from the parents of the youth. Even if you choose to teach the principles of type without using an instrument, it is important to inform the parents that you are doing so. There is just enough distrust of "psychological instruments" that you may get into serious conflict if you do not give full information to the parents.

The Challenge of Pastoral Care

In any pastoral-care setting, type can help caregivers evaluate their own strengths and weaknesses. Type can help the caregiver understand the most important ways to compensate for those weaknesses.

In addition, type can help us minister to people in ways that are most effective for them. Sometimes we know their types; sometimes we do not. Understanding the framework of type can enable us to ask a variety of questions that draw on each of the type preferences, thus helping us to minister to people who are different than we are. And that includes just about everybody!

CHAPTER 9

A Warning
and a Word of Encouragement

I have tried to present a wide variety of ways that type can be used in congregations, keeping in mind Isabel Briggs Myers' passion for the constructive use of differences. Understanding our differences through the positive lens of type can help us—congregation members, lay leaders, and clergy—work together more effectively.

After laying out all these ways of using type, I want to point out that in any congregation it would be best to start with only one or two of these options. If we try to use type in every possible setting, and if we talk about it too much, people will begin to think we have embraced a new gospel.

I look at just about everything through the lens of type, but I try to be very careful how much I talk about it. I have been using type in my own congregation for several years by leading an annual workshop on finding a place to serve. That is the only formal way I use type right now. I was ordained fairly recently, and I haven't done any weddings yet. I expect to use type in pre-marriage counseling. I mention type occasionally in meetings or conversations when it seems particularly pertinent, but I am very reluctant to talk about type frequently. Many people are offended by categorization of any kind. I don't want to get in the way of their faith.

If you are new to type and enthusiastic about using it, please heed my warning to go slowly. Observe and think a lot before you speak. Find one or two interested friends with whom to share your observations. Pick one area of congregational life in which to teach type principles. Work on bringing type principles into conversations without using type vocabulary. ("I think we need to gather more data before making this decision" instead of "We've skimped on getting sensing information." "I wish we could be more attentive to the needs of our neighborhood" rather than "Our congregation is so introverted.")

A Personal Challenge

If you read this book because of the subtitle, "How To Work With Others More Effectively," I want to encourage you to use type first and foremost to grow in understanding yourself. Self-knowledge is the first key to working productively with others.

Type can help you understand the way you come across to other people. The judging-perceiving preference, for example, can help you understand the extent to which you appear to be either rigid or overly unstructured as you work with others.

Type can help you understand and accept your energy level in various settings. The extravert-introvert preference can illuminate what you need in order to function in an energized fashion. This has great impact on relationships in which you are working together.

The sensing-intuition preference can help you understand the kind of information you need. Understanding that preference can help you ask for what you need in a gentle way.

The thinking-feeling preference can help you understand your priorities. Again, you will be able to ask more clearly and more kindly for what you need if you understand this preference.

If you have a preference for introversion, type will help you see the way you come across to the world through your auxiliary function, which is extraverted. Your dominant function will be introverted, hidden from the world, yet it will be the most important arena of functioning for you. You will come to appreciate the kind of misunderstandings that arise from this simple fact, and you will be able to be more proactive to avoid confusion.

I'll use my own type as an illustration. My dominant function, introverted intuition, is hidden inside me. It is a flexible, exploring function, always seeking new insights and continuously exploring new ideas. But I meet the world with my auxiliary function, extraverted thinking. I often come across as rigid and overly organized, which is not at all what's happening inside. When I meet new people with whom I'm going to be working, I have learned to say, "I often seem to have made up my mind about things, and I talk about my opinions readily. I want you to know that deep inside, I'm always open to new information, so feel free to tell me anything. Don't be afraid to disagree with me. I sound more opinionated than I really am."

If you have a preference for extraversion, type can help you understand your need to process information out loud. It is immensely helpful for an extravert to be able to say in meetings, "I'm thinking out loud right now. Don't hold me to what I've just said! Let's interact some more about this issue before we decide."

I encourage you to go back to chapter 5 and re-read it in the light of working with others. In that chapter I tried to show some of the ways type can help us grow in self-acceptance. Our issues of insecurity and self-doubt greatly affect our working relationships within congregations because we can project our weaknesses onto others if we aren't conscious of what's going on. If we grow in our awareness of our path toward self-acceptance, we will be better able to avoid some judgmentalism and some conflict.

In chapter 5, I also tried to express some of the ways type can help us access the power and potential of our shadow. When we are at our weakest, such as when we are under stress, we may find ourselves in the grip of our inferior function. This can be an opportunity for growth in self-understanding. This can also help us explore some of the lost opportunities and undeveloped potential that usually lie hidden in our shadow. This process of growth will enable us to work better with others because we won't be blindsided so often by the emergence of these powerful feelings that can overwhelm us and make us very difficult to be with and work with.

Type is a wonderful tool to help us understand group dynamics and to help us cope with the great differences among people. Type can also help us grow in understanding ourselves, an understanding which builds an ongoing foundation for working effectively with others.

I wish you joy and peace in your journey of faith, and I hope that type will help you along the way.

Books on Type
for Use in Congregations

Type and Spirituality

Grant, W. Harold; Magdala Thompson; and Thomas E. Clarke. *From Image to Likeness: A Jungian Path in the Gospel Journey*. New York: Paulist Press, 1983.
Four major chapters describe patterns of spirituality based on each of the four functions. In Appendix B Grant presents a theory of type development over life which has become widely accepted in the type community.

Hirsh, Sandra Krebs and Jane A. G. Kise. *Looking at Type and Spirituality*. Gainesville, Fla.: Center for Applications of Psychological Type, 1997.
Patterns of spirituality for each of the type preferences are presented, along with a description of what spirituality often looks like for each of the 16 types.

Johnson, Reginald. *Your Personality and God*. Wheaton, Ill.: Victor Books, 1988. (Originally published with the title *Celebrate My Soul*.)
The bulk of the book is eight chapters based on the eight dominant functions (ES, IS, EN, IN, ET, IT, EF, IF). Johnson presents one biblical character to illustrate each dominant function, then describes giftedness, infirmities, nurture, and growth for each one.

Pearson, Mark A. *Why Can't I Be Me?* Grand Rapids, Mich.: Chosen Books, 1992.

Presents the implications of type in three areas of spiritual life: emotional healing, relationship/teamwork, and spiritual growth. Lots of stories to illustrate author's points.

Richardson, Peter Tufts. *Four Spiritualities*. Palo Alto, Calif.: Davies-Black Publishing, 1996.
Richardson uses the four function pairs to lay out four different spiritual pathways in world religions (NT—Journey of Unity, SF—Journey of Devotion, ST—Journey of Works, and NF—Journey of Harmony). He draws on many religious traditions from all over the world, illustrating each of the four pathways with myriad quotations.

Type and Prayer

Duncan, Bruce. *Pray Your Way: Your Personality and God*. London: Darton, Longman and Todd, 1993. Distributed in the USA by Abingdon.
Duncan describes the ways that all type preferences can be found in God. He describes prayer patterns based on each of the eight functions (ES, IS, EN, IN, ET, IT, EF, IF). He believes that we will have a preferred, everyday prayer pattern based on our dominant function, but our deepest experiences of God will come out of our less-preferred functions.

Michael, Chester P. and Marie C. Norrisey. *Prayer and Temperament: Different Prayer Forms for Different Personality Types*. Charlottesville, Va: The Open Door, 1984.
An early book on type and prayer. Each of the four temperaments (SJ, NF, SF, NT) is linked with a classic Christian prayer form (Ignatian, Augustinian, Franciscan, and Thomistic). The section on *lectio divina* shows how *lectio divina* draws on all four functions.

Type and Service

Harbaugh, Gary. *God's Gifted People: Discovering Your Personality as a Gift*. Minneapolis: Augsburg, 1990.

Harbaugh uses the four function pairs to present patterns of Christian service (ST—the gift of practicality, SF—the gift of personal helpfulness, NF—the gift of possibilities for people, and NT—the gift of looking ahead). He uses a story of four individuals that runs throughout the book.

Kise, Jane A. G.; David Stark and Sandra Krebs Hirsh. *LifeKeys*. Minneapolis: Bethany House, 1996.
Psychological type is one of several tools described in this book to help people find a place to serve. Others include spiritual gifts, values, and passions. The authors present clear teaching plans for using the material in adult classes in congregations and for retreats.

Type and Congregations

Edwards, Lloyd. *How We Belong, Fight, and Pray*. Washington, D.C.: the Alban Institute, 1993.
A brief and practical book presenting issues concerning type for leadership boards and other church activities.

Oswald, Roy M. and Otto Kroeger. *Personality Type and Religious Leadership*. Washington, D.C.: the Alban Institute: 1988.
The authors present research from congregations regarding type patterns among Christian clergy (lots of NFs) and congregations (lots of SJs). There are interesting differences in patterns among denominations.

Other Helpful Books

Barger, Nancy J. and Linda K. Kirby. *Type and Change*. Palo Alto, Ca.: Consulting Psychologists Press, 1997.
A workbook for navigating change in organizations, with discussion questions and profiles of the impact of change on each of the 16 types.

Bridges, William. *The Character of Organizations: Using Jungian Type in Organizational Development*. Palo Alto, Calif.: Davies-Black Publishing, 1992.

Bridges believes that organizations have types, and that responses in stress, loss, and change can be related to type. His "Organizational Character Index," found in an appendix, is not a validated instrument, but it has lots of interesting and helpful questions to use in determining an organization's type.

Corlett, Eleanor S. and Nancy B. Millner. *Navigating Midlife: Using Typology as a Guide*. Palo Alto, Ca.: Consulting Psychologists Press Books, 1993.
According to the authors, midlife raises issues of meaning and values which are closely related to spirituality. Many aspects of midlife that are presented relate to spiritual questions.

Ginn, Charles W., *Voices of Loss*. Gainesville, Fla.: Center for Applications of Psychological Type, 1994.
Each of the 16 types is represented in a story of loss that describes common patterns for that type.

Hartzler, Margaret and Gary Hartzler. *Using Type With Couples*. Gaithersburg, Md.: Type Resources.
Contains a checklist of potential strengths and problems for all possible type pairings in marriage (extravert-extravert, extravert-introvert, introvert-introvert, etc.). The address and phone number for Type Resources are: 101 Chestnut Street, #135, Gaithersburg, MD 20877, 301-840-8575.

Hirsh, Sandra Krebs with Jane A. G. Kise. *Work It Out: Clues for Solving People Problems at Work*. Palo Alto, Ca.: Davies-Black Publishing, 1996.
Using a series of case studies, the authors present the impact of type in work conflict situations.

Kroeger, Otto with Janet M. Thuesen. *Type Talk at Work*. New York: Delacorte Press, 1992.
A guide to using type in the workplace to identify your own work style and work more effectively with others.

Lawrence, Gordon. *Looking at Type and Learning Styles*. Gainesville, Fla.: Center for Applications of Psychological Type, 1997.

A clear presentation of the implications of type in the classroom and in other learning situations. Much of the material in this 56-page book is a distillation of Lawrence's 1977 book *People Types and Tiger Stripes*.

Myers, Isabel Briggs with Peter B. Myers. *Gifts Differing*. Palo Alto, Calif.: Consulting Psychologists Press, 1980.
The first and most insightful book on the basics of type. Isabel Briggs Myers developed the Myers-Briggs Type Indicator, and this book reflects her understanding of the nuances of type.

Penley, Janet P. and Diane W. Stephens. *The M.O.M.S. Handbook: Understanding Your Personality Type in Mothering*. Wilmette, Ill.: Mothers of Many Styles, 1995.
By the founders of the organization Mothers of Many Styles. Hints, tips, and common mothering patterns are presented based on issues of type. The address and phone number of the organization are 604 Maple Ave., Wilmette. IL 60091, 847-251-4936.

Quenk, Naomi L. *Beside Ourselves: Our Hidden Personalities in Everyday Life*. Palo Alto, Ca.: Consulting Psychologists Press, 1993.
Quenk does not address spirituality directly in this book, yet the emergence of the inferior function has deeply spiritual implications. Her book vividly describes what it looks like for the inferior function to come to the surface when we least expect it, which is a first step in exploring the spiritual significance of the inferior function.

Tieger, Paul D. and Barbara Barron-Tieger. *Nurture by Nature: Understand Your Child's Personality Type—And Become a Better Parent*. Boston: Little, Brown and Co., 1997.
Presents the needs of children based on personality type.

Introduction
1. Chester P. Michael and Marie C. Norrisey, *Prayer and Temperament* (Charlottesville, Va: The Open Door, 1984).
2. In one book, *Born to Rebel: Birth Order, Family Dynamics, and Creative Lives* (New York: Pantheon Books, 1996), Frank J. Sulloway studies scientists who brought about great paradigm shifts in scientific theory. Almost none of them was a firstborn or only child.
3. David Kiersey and Marilyn Bates, *Please Understand Me* (Del Mar, Calif.: Prometheus Nemesis Book Company, 1984).
4. Isabel Briggs Myers with Peter B. Myers, *Gifts Differing* (Palo Alto, Calif.: Consulting Psychologists Press, 1980).

Chapter 1
1. C. G. Jung, *Psychological Types* (Princeton, N. J.: Princeton University Press, 1971).
2. Available from Consulting Psychologists Press, Inc., 1-800-624-1765.
3. Available from Human Resource Dimensions, Inc., 400 Birchfield Drive, Suite 400, Mount Laurel, N.J. 08054.
4. Jung, *Psychological Types*, 333-337.
5. Ibid., 373-378.
6. Allen L. Hammer and Wayne D. Mitchell, "The Distribution of MBTI Types in the U.S. by Gender and Ethnic Group," *Journal of Psychological Type* 37 (1996), 7.
7. Jung, *Psychological Types*, 362.
8. Ibid., 366.
9. Roy M. Oswald and Otto Kroeger, *Personality Type and Reli-*

gious Leadership (Washington, D.C.: the Alban Institute, 1988), 22.

10. Jung, *Psychological Types*, 342, 354.

11. Isabel Briggs Myers with Peter B. Myers, *Gifts Differing*, 8, 9.

12. Bruce Duncan, *Pray Your Way: Your Personality and God* (London: Darton, Longman and Todd, 1993), 55-62.

13. Ibid., 57.

14. Ibid., 57, 58

15. Ibid., 58.

16. Ibid., 59.

17. Ibid., 59, 60.

18. Ibid., 60.

19. Ibid., 61.

20. Ibid., 61, 62.

21. Gary Harbaugh, *God's Gifted People: Discovering Your Personality as a Gift* (Minneapolis: Augsburg, 1990). These are the chapter headings of chapters 3 through 6.

22. Peter Tufts Richardson, *Four Spiritualities: Expressions of Self, Expressions of Spirit* (Palo Alto, Calif.: Davies-Black Publishing, 1996). These are the chapter headings of chapters 4 through 7.

23. Kiersey and Bates, *Please Understand Me*, 27-66.

24. Michael and Norrisey, *Prayer and Temperament*.

25. Duncan, *Pray Your Way*, 98-125.

26. W. Harold Grant, Magdala Thompson, and Thomas E. Clarke, *From Image to Likeness: A Jungian Path in the Gospel Journey* (New York: Paulist Press, 1983). These are the chapter titles of chapters 2 through 5.

Chapter 2

1. Eleanor S. Corlett and Nancy B. Millner, *Navigating Midlife: Using Typology as a Guide* (Palo Alto, Calif.: Consulting Psychologists Press Books, 1993), 7.

2. Harbaugh, *God's Gifted People*, 61.

3. You may want to consult the book *LifeKeys* by Jane A. G. Kise, Gary Stark, and Sandra Krebs Hirsh (Minneapolis: Bethany House, 1996). The subtitle of their book is "Discovering who you are, why you're here and what you do best." Spiritual gifts and psychological type are accompanied with values, passions, and life choices to help people find a direction for service. An appendix in their book gives several formats for retreats and courses using their material.

Chapter 3

1. C. Peter Wagner, *Your Spiritual Gifts Can Help Your Church Grow* (Ventura, Calif.: Regal Books, 1979).

2. Don and Katie Fortune, *Discover Your God-Given Gifts* (Old Tappan, N.J.: Fleming Revell, 1987).

3. Harbaugh, *God's Gifted People*, 11-17.

Chapter 4

1. Grant, Thompson, and Clarke, *From Image to Likeness*.

2. Michael and Norrisey, *Prayer and Temperament*.

3. Isabel Briggs Myers with Peter B. Myers, *Gifts Differing*, 8, 9.

4. Reginald Johnson, *Your Personality and God* (Wheaton, Ill.: Victor Books, 1988), 53, 54.

5. Ibid., 63.

6. Duncan, *Pray Your Way*, 108.

7. Ibid., 116.

8. Michael and Norrisey, *Prayer and Temperament*, 32.

9. Ibid., 34.

Chapter 5

1. Heidi J. Dalzell, "Eating Disorders: Beyond the Persona," *Bulletin of Psychological Type* 20, No. 4 (Autumn 1997): 1, 3.

2. Grant, Thompson, and Clarke, *From Image to Likeness*, 215-248.

3. Jung, *Psychological Types*.

4. Developed by June Singer, Mary Loomis, Elizabeth Kirkhart, and Larry Kirkhart. Copyright 1996 by Moving Boundaries, Inc., 1375 S.W. Blaine Court, Gresham, Oreg. 97080.

5. Naomi Quenk, *Beside Ourselves: Our Hidden Personalities in Everyday Life* (Palo Alto, Calif.: Consulting Psychologists Press, 1993).

6. Corlett and Millner, *Navigating Midlife*, 1.

7. Peter Malone made this statement at the Religious and Spiritual Issues Symposium at the International Association for Psychological Type conference in July, 1997.

Chapter 6

1. Gordon Lawrence, *Looking at Type and Learning Styles* (Gainesville, Fla.: Center for Applications of Psychological Type, 1997), 15.

2. Ibid., 14.

3. Sandra Krebs Hirsh and Jane A. G. Kise, *Looking at Type and Spirituality* (Gainesville, Fla.: Center for Applications of Psychological Type, 1997), 13.

4. Ibid.

5. Lawrence, *Type and Learning Styles*, 12.

6. Ibid.

7. Duncan, *Pray Your Way*, 61, 62.

Chapter 7

1. Some of the material about using the four functions in decision-making comes from Sandra Krebs Hirsh with Jane A. G. Kise, *Work It Out: Clues for Solving People Problems at Work* (Palo Alto, Calif.: Davies-Black Publishing, 1996), 257, 258.

2. William Bridges, *The Character of Organizations: Using Jungian Type in Organizational Development* (Palo Alto, Calif.: Davies-Black Publishing, 1992), 6, 7.

3. These characteristics are adapted from an unpublished questionnaire by Alban Institute Senior Consultant Roy Oswald and from William Bridges' "Organizational Character Index" in *The Character of Organizations*, 115-119.

4. Bridges, *The Character of Organizations*, 110.

5. Nancy Barger and Linda Kirby, *Type and Change* (Palo Alto, Calif.: Consulting Psychologists Press, 1997), 16.

6. Ibid.

7. Ibid.

8. Ibid.

9. The needs of each preference are adapted from Barger and Kirby, *Type and Change*, 7.

10. Bridges, *The Character of Organizations*, 64.

11. Ibid.

12. Ibid., 65.

13. Ibid.

14. Ibid., 66.

15. Ibid., 67.

Chapter 8

1. Charles W. Ginn, *Voices of Loss* (Gainesville, Fla: Center for Applications of Psychological Type, 1994), 13.

2. Ibid., 17.

3. Margaret Hartzler and Gary Hartzler, *Using Type With Couples* (Gaithersburg, Md.: Type Resources), III-5.

4. Janet P. Penley and Diane W. Stephens, *The M.O.M.S. Handbook: Understanding Your Personality Type in Mothering* (Wilmette, Ill.: Mothers of Many Styles, 1995), 36.

5. Paul D. Tieger and Barbara Barron-Tieger, *Nurture by Nature: Understand Your Child's Personality Type—And Become a Better Parent* (Boston: Little, Brown and Co., 1997).